CONDUCTOR

ESSENTIAL ELEMENTS
FOR JAZZ ENSEMBLE
Book 2

A COMPREHENSIVE METHOD FOR JAZZ STYLE AND IMPROVISATION

By MIKE STEINEL

Managing Editor:
MICHAEL SWEENEY

THREE BASIC SECTIONS

I. **Daily Drills, Warm-ups, and Workouts**
II. **Improvisation Lessons**
III. **Performance Spotlights (Repertoire)**

Includes Teacher Guidance and Lesson Plans (pp. 8 – 9)

This book is the second in a series and is designed for developing musicians and ensembles. The first book: ***Essential Elements for Jazz Ensemble*** is a comprehensive introduction to the jazz style, theory, improvisation and history. The exercises and compositions in this book can be played by a full jazz ensemble, combo, or individually with the recordings. The nine compositions for full band cover a variety of styles, tempos, and keys, and include Demonstration Solos for study and reference.

The recordings are available as a free download. Visit www.halleonard.com/mylibrary and use the code printed below to access your mp3s.

We hope you find this book helpful, and always remember…have fun playing jazz.

To access audio visit:
www.halleonard.com/mylibrary
Enter Code
"J2CN-0638-1633-9313"

ISBN 978-1-4950-7902-3

Copyright © 2019 by HAL LEONARD LLC
International Copyright Secured All Rights Reserved

7777 W. Bluemound Rd. P.O. Box 13819 Milwaukee, WI 53213

TABLE OF CONTENTS

Overview of ESSENTIAL ELEMENTS FOR JAZZ ENSEMBLE BOOK 2

ESSENTIAL ELEMENTS FOR JAZZ ENSEMBLE BOOK 2 is for intermediate level musicians and ensembles. Like the first book (ESSENTIAL ELEMENTS FOR JAZZ ENSEMBLE), it features drills, exercises, lessons and repertoire that address more advanced elements of jazz style, theory, improvisation, and history. Through nine original Spotlight Performance tunes, students will explore the epicenters of jazz, recreating the distinctive styles of The Big Easy and The Windy City to the sounds of Beale Street, Vine Street, Baytown and more. As Ken Burn's *Jazz* documentary famously says: "Jazz was born in New Orleans, but grew up everywhere else."

Enjoy the trip! Mike Steinel

About the author

Mike Steinel is a jazz trumpeter, pianist, composer and arranger. An internationally recognized jazz educator, he has performed throughout the U.S., Canada, and in Europe and Asia. He has recorded with the Rosewood Trio, the Frank Mantooth Orchestra, the Chicago Jazz Quintet and is a featured soloist on recent releases by the Mike Waldrop Big Band (2015 and 2018).

Steinel's CD *Song And Dance,* released on Origin Records in 2018, features The Mike Steinel Jazz Quintet performing all original material (music and lyrics by Steinel). He has performed with Ella Fitzgerald, Clark Terry, Don Ellis, Bill Evans, Zoot Sims, Jerry Bergonzi, and others. Mike served as Professor of Jazz Studies at the University of North Texas from 1987 to 2019. He founded then directed the UNT Jazz Combo Workshop for 28 years. Mike served as Co-Chair of the Jazz Advisory Panel for the National Endowment for the Arts. He holds a BME degree from Emporia State University and a MME degree from the University of North Texas.

Acknowledgements

The preparation of this book would not have been possible without significant contributions from Mike Sweeney, Jim Gagne, Bruce Bush, Paul Lavender, and Steve Smith. I thank them, and all of the kind folks at Hal Leonard Corporation, for giving me the opportunity to create the next level of what we sincerely hope is a meaningful contribution to the field of jazz education.

Thank you, friends

I wish to thank the many educators and musicians who offered suggestions and ideas during the development of ESSENTIAL ELEMENTS FOR JAZZ ENSEMBLE BOOK 2: Steve Barnes, John Murphy, Lynn Seaton, Brian Piper, Tony Baker, Devin Eddleman, Paul Metzger, and Rosana Eckert. A special note of gratitude goes to my wife, Beverly Hoch, for her work proof-reading the method. I am profoundly grateful to our engineer Eric Delegard at Reel Time Audio (Denton, TX) who recorded and mastered the play-along tracks.

Who should use ESSENTIAL ELEMENTS FOR JAZZ ENSEMBLE BOOK 2?

This book can be used with ensembles or individually. Even though it is not an introductory method, a brief review section summarizes the information contained in ESSENTIAL ELEMENTS FOR JAZZ ENSEMBLE. It will be most productive if students have studied the material in Book 1 thoroughly and have a basic command of major scales, basic seventh chords, key signatures, and blues scales before attempting the material in this book. Each numbered exercise is accompanied by a recorded track to be downloaded using an individual activation code printed on the title page of each book.

How to use ESSENTIAL ELEMENTS FOR JAZZ ENSEMBLE BOOK 2

The Three Basic Sections:

1) Daily Drills, Warm-ups, and Workouts
2) Improvisation Lessons
3) Nine Performance Spotlights (Repertoire)

allow the director flexibility to adjust the content to the needs of their ensemble and the limitations of their rehearsal time. Even though the tunes become more advanced as the book progresses, educators may find it more advantageous to present material "out of sequence." Sample lesson plans are included.

Original Tunes in ESSENTIAL ELEMENTS FOR JAZZ ENSEMBLE BOOK 2 by Mike Steinel

The Saints Are Swingin' Low
Vine Street Ruckus
Beale Street Barbeque
Windy City
Baytown Boogaloo
Liberty Bell Shuffle
Ipanema Dreamin'
Skating in the Park
Five's a Crowd

1) Daily Drills, Warm-Ups, and Workouts

Exercises selected from Student Book Pages 4 through 15 should be played at the beginning of each practice session.

Page 4: The **Basic Scale and Style Workouts** reinforce the keys or modes of the Performance Spotlights (repertoire): F Major, F Mixolydian, B♭ Mixolydian, C Dorian, E♭ Major, and G Minor (Harmonic Minor). These should be played as part of a daily workout until mastered.

Pages 5-6: **Rhythm Workouts for Reading and Style** are progressive. Two or three exercises could be included in each session.

Page 7: **Jazz Expression Workouts** are challenging and should be included in each rehearsal until mastered. Review and reinforce them often since these characteristic expressions and gestures appear in the Performance Spotlights.

Page 8: **Warm-Ups for Balance, Blend and Intonation** can be used to prepare for each repertoire piece. Have various sections play the exercises alone to identify and correct weaknesses.

Pages 9-11: **Major, Mixolydian, and Dorian by the Numbers** patterns can be used with any major scale, mixolydian mode, or dorian mode, and train students to think more theoretically.

Pages 12-15: **Pentatonic and Blues Workouts** can be used to prepare particularly bluesy repertoire such as *Vine Street Rumble, Liberty Bell Blues, Windy City,* and *Beale Street Barbeque.*

Performance Spotlights (full band arrangements) are preceded by rhythm workouts, melody workouts and improvisation lessons.

Sample Rehearsal Schedule (50 minutes)

One exercise from page 4 (Scale/Style Workout) = 1 min.

Two exercises from pages 5 and 6 (for Reading) = 2 min.

Two exercise from page 7 (Jazz Expression) = 2 min.

One exercise from page 8 (Balance/Blend/Intonation) repeated 2xs = 1 min.

Two exercises from pages 9 – 11 (Scales/Modes by Numbers) = 2 min.

Two exercises from pages 12 – 15 (Pentatonics/Blues Scales) = 2 min.

Improvisation Lesson = 5 to 10 minutes

Performance Spotlights/Repertoire = 30 to 35 min.

2) Improvisation Lessons

Lesson #1 – Reinventing Melody introduces students to the most basic and simplest form of improvisation: melodic paraphrase. The techniques can and should be applied to any melody a student chooses.

Lesson #2 – Ornamenting Melody provides examples of basic ornamentation. This is more theoretically based and may require some review of scale/chord relationships.

Lesson #3 – Blues Riffs demonstrates how short bluesy melodies (riffs) can be used over a blues progression.

Lesson #4 – Call and Response details one of the most common melodic constructions in jazz.

Lessons #5 – Mixolydian Vamp and Chromatic Passing Tones shows how melodies can be more interesting when extra notes are added to basic scales.

Lesson #6 – Chromatic Passing Tones and the Composite Blues Scale organizes common passing tones into a scale construction.

Lesson #7 – Triplets in Swing and Dorian Vamp introduces the modes of the major scale and triplet rhythms.

Lesson #8 – Dorian Vamp and Minor Pentatonic Scale is a good warm up for soloing on "Windy City."

Lesson #9 – Bebop Scale and Lick, Double Time Playing introduces one very common jazz scale that contains chromaticism.

Lesson #10 – Double Time and the Ten Note Bebop Scale adds a variation to the material in lesson #9.

Lesson #11 – 9th Chords and Chord Tone Soloing introduces common chord extensions and typical chord tone vocabulary.

Lesson #12 – Chromatics and Passing Tones demonstrates many common chromatic embellishments of basic 9th chords.

Lesson #13 – ii-V in Major and Minor introduces the most common progression in jazz.

Lesson #14 – Scale Bracketing over the ii-V-I shows how one scale can be applied to many chords in a progression.

Guidelines for Performance Spotlights

The tunes in *Essential Elements for Jazz Ensemble Book 2* represent nine distinctive "regional aspects" of American jazz music. Directors can take advantage of these style varieties and provide additional listening and videos as suggested below. Outcome: the student can begin to recognize the sounds of each region.

Sample Lesson Plans

First Semester

Week 1 – 4
Daily Drills, Warm-Ups and Workouts
- Select one or two exercises from Page 4 – 8 each day
- Select exercises from Page 9 (in F) each day
- Alternate between Lesson #1 and #2

Performance Spotlight – ***The Saints are Swingin' Low***
Listening/Video – Ken Burns Jazz – Episode 1

Week 5 – 8
Daily Drills, Warm-Ups and Workouts
- Select exercises from Page 4 – 8 each day
- Select exercises from Page 10 (in F) each day
- Select exercises from 13 and 15 each day
- Alternate between Lesson #3 and #4

Performance Spotlight – ***Vine Street Ruckus***
Listening/Video – Ken Burns Jazz – Episode 5
Review – Lesson #1 and #2
Review – *The Saints are Swingin' Low*

Week 9 – 12
Daily Drills, Warm-Ups and Workouts
- Select exercises from Page 4 – 8 each day
- Select exercises from Page 10 (in B♭) each day
- Select exercises from 12 and 14 each day

Alternate between Lesson #5 and #6
Performance Spotlight - ***Beale Street Barbeque***
Listening – *Memphis Underground* by Herbie Mann
Review – Lesson #3 and #4
Review – *Vine Street Ruckus*

Week 13 – 16
Daily Drills, Warm-Ups and Workouts
- Select exercises from Page 4 – 8 each day
- Select exercises from Page 11 each day
- Alternate between Lesson #7 and #8

Performance Spotlight – ***Windy City***
Listening – *Tanya* by Dexter Gordon
Review – Lesson #5 and #6
Review – *Beale Street Barbeque*

Note: Add additional repertoire each day as time permits.

Second Semester

Week 1 – 4
Daily Drills, Warm-Ups and Workouts
- Select exercises from Page 4 – 8 each day
- Select exercises from Page 10 (In F) each day
- Select exercises from 13 and 15 each day
- Alternate between Lesson #9 and #10

Performance Spotlight – ***Baytown Boogaloo***
Listening – *Soul Vaccination* by Tower of Power
Review – Lesson #7 and #8
Review – *Windy City*

Week 5 – 8
Daily Drills, Warm-Ups and Workouts
- Select exercises from Page 4 – 8 each day
- Select exercises from Page 10 each day
- Select exercises from 12 and 14 each day
- Alternate between Lesson #11 and #12

Performance Spotlight – ***Liberty Bell Shuffle***
Listening – *Blue Train* by John Coltrane
Review – Lesson #9 and #10
Review – *Baytown Boogaloo*

Week 9 – 12
Daily Drills, Warm-Ups and Workouts
- Select exercises from Page 4 – 8 each day
- Select exercises from Page 10 each day
- Select exercises from 12 and 14 each day
- Alternate between Lesson #11 and #12

Performance Spotlight – ***Ipanema Dreamin'***
Listening – *Autumn Leaves* by Miles Davis
Listening – *Girl from Ipanema* by Stan Getz
Review – Lesson #11 and #12
Review – *Liberty Bell Shuffle*

Week 13 – 16
Daily Drills, Warm-Ups and Workouts
- Select exercises from Page 4 – 8 each day
- Select exercises from Page 11 each day
- Select exercises from 12 and 14 each day
- Alternate between Lesson #13 and #14

Performance Spotlight – ***Skating In The Park***
Performance Spotlight – ***Five's A Crowd***
Listening – *Skating in Central Park* by The Modern Jazz Quartet
Listening – *Take Five* by Dave Brubeck Quartet
Review – *Ipanema Dreamin'*

THE BASICS OF JAZZ STYLE

Review from *Essential Elements for Jazz Ensemble* (Book 1)

Jazz Articulation Review

These are the four basic articulations in jazz and the related scat syllables for each. "Doo", "Bah", "Dit" and "Dot" can be used to remind us (aurally) of the sound. However, these are not necessarily how we will articulate on the individual instruments.

Attacks and Releases

In traditional music you use a "Tah" articulation to begin a note and taper the note at the end.

In jazz it is common to use a "Doo" attack (soft and legato) to begin a note. It is also common to end the note with the tongue. This "tongue-stop" gives the music a rhythmic feeling.

Accenting "2 and 4"

For most traditional music the important beats in 4/4 time are 1 and 3. In jazz, however, the emphasis is usually on beats 2 and 4. Emphasizing "2 and 4" gives the music a jazz feeling.

Quarter Notes

In swing style quarter notes are usually played detached. In Latin or Rock they may be played with a variety of articulations but are often played full value.

Swing 8th Notes Sound Different Than They Look

In swing the 2nd 8th note of each beat is actually played like the last third of a triplet, and slightly accented. 8th notes in swing style are usually played legato.

8ths in Latin and Rock (Straight 8th Music)

8th Notes in Latin or Rock are played evenly and the articulations are often quite different than in swing style.

Jazz Ornamentation and Expression

There are many ornaments and articulations which are associated with jazz and necessary to achieve a characteristic jazz feeling. These are the most common:

Bend:
Start the note on pitch, lower it momentarily, then return to original pitch.

Scoop:
Slide into the note from below pitch. Scoops can be executed with the embouchure or the fingers or a combination of both.

Plop:
Slide down to a note from above slightly before the note is to be played. Plops can be short or long.

Fall:
At the end of the note let the pitch fall off. Falls may be executed with the embouchure or the fingers or a combination of both. Falls can be short or long.

Doit:
Slide the pitch upwards at the end of the note.

Glissando:
Slide from one note to the next smoothly. Glissandos may be executed with the embouchure or the fingers or a combination of both.

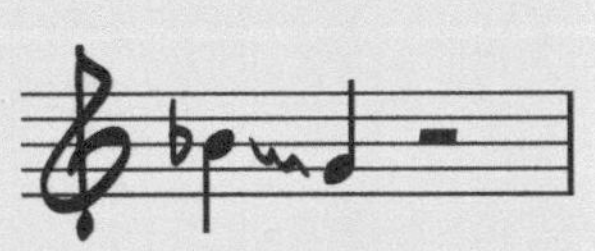

Flip
Often called a turn, the flip is executed by quickly playing a note above the original note (usually a step or half step), returning to the original note and then proceeding to the next written note.

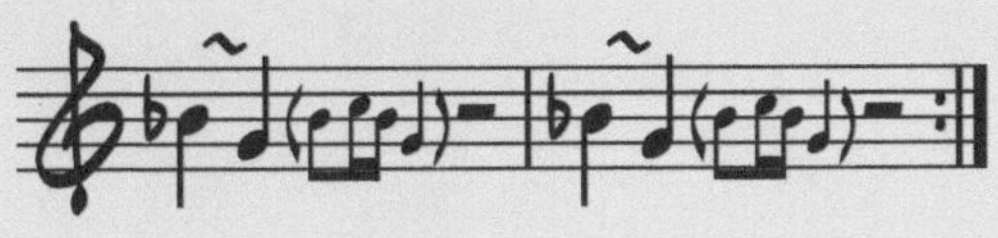

BASIC JAZZ THEORY AND IMPROVISATION

Review from *Essential Elements for Jazz Ensemble* (Book 1)

Chord and Scale Review

Chord Type	Chord Symbol	Related Scale or Mode for Improvisation
Major Seventh	B♭MA7	*B♭ Major Scale*
Dominant Seventh	B♭7	*B♭ Mixolydian Mode* — Note: the Blues Scale can be used with Dominant Seventh Chords, Minor Seventh Chords, and the entire Blues Progression — *B♭ Blues Scale*
Minor Seventh	B♭MI7	*B♭ Dorian Mode* — *B♭ Blues Scale*

The Dominant Seventh Chord is a "jazzy" chord

Because of its flattened seventh (often called a "blue note") the **Dominant Seventh Chord** has a very "jazzy" or "bluesy" sound.

The Blues Progression

The harmony of a jazz song is called the chord progression. The most common chord progression in jazz is the blues. Usually the blues is a twelve-bar repeated pattern using three **Dominant Seventh Chords**. The roots (bottom notes) of these three chords are usually the first, fourth, and fifth notes of the key of the blues.

Common Blues Progression in B♭ using Dominant Chords and Mixolydian Modes

Common Blues Progression in F using Dominant Chords and Mixolydian Modes

Two Common Blues Scales (Minor and Major)

Minor and Major Blues Scales in B♭

Minor and Major Blues Scales in F

Drums Only

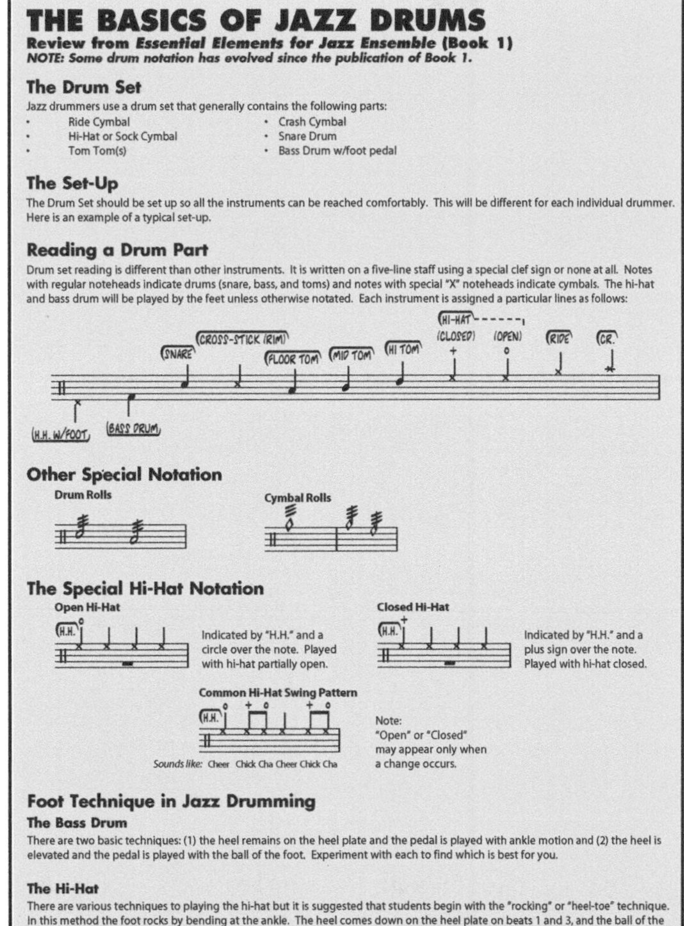

THE BASICS OF JAZZ DRUMS

Review from *Essential Elements for Jazz Ensemble* (Book 1)
NOTE: Some drum notation has evolved since the publication of Book 1.

The Drum Set

Jazz drummers use a drum set that generally contains the following parts:

- Ride Cymbal
- Hi-Hat or Sock Cymbal
- Tom Tom(s)
- Crash Cymbal
- Snare Drum
- Bass Drum w/foot pedal

The Set-Up

The Drum Set should be set up so all the instruments can be reached comfortably. This will be different for each individual drummer. Here is an example of a typical set-up.

Reading a Drum Part

Drum set reading is different than other instruments. It is written on a five-line staff using a special clef sign or none at all. Notes with regular noteheads indicate drums (snare, bass, and toms) and notes with special "X" noteheads indicate cymbals. The hi-hat and bass drum will be played by the feet unless otherwise notated. Each instrument is assigned a particular lines as follows:

Other Special Notation

Drum Rolls

Cymbal Rolls

The Special Hi-Hat Notation

Open Hi-Hat

Indicated by "H.H." and a circle over the note. Played with hi-hat partially open.

Closed Hi-Hat

Indicated by "H.H." and a plus sign over the note. Played with hi-hat closed.

Common Hi-Hat Swing Pattern

Sounds like: Cheer Chick Cha Cheer Chick Cha

Note:
"Open" or "Closed" may appear only when a change occurs.

Foot Technique in Jazz Drumming

The Bass Drum

There are two basic techniques: (1) the heel remains on the heel plate and the pedal is played with ankle motion and (2) the heel is elevated and the pedal is played with the ball of the foot. Experiment with each to find which is best for you.

The Hi-Hat

There are various techniques to playing the hi-hat but it is suggested that students begin with the "rocking" or "heel-toe" technique. In this method the foot rocks by bending at the ankle. The heel comes down on the heel plate on beats 1 and 3, and the ball of the foot comes down on the pedal on beats 2 and 4. This produces a crisp hi-hat "chick" on beats 2 and 4 and is a fundamental part of playing the basic swing pattern.

The Ride Cymbal

In jazz marked "swing" the ride cymbal reinforces the quarter note walking bass line provided by the bass player. These two instruments supply the rhythmic foundation of swing music.

The Basic Ride Cymbal Pattern

The ride cymbal pattern is usually played in a triplet feel, however it is not always strict. At slow tempos the pattern is very triplety but at faster tempos the eighth notes are played more evenly. In this book we will always notate the ride pattern in eighth notes.

The basic Ride Cymbal Pattern is notated as:

The basic Ride Cymbal Pattern sounds like:

The Basic Swing Pattern – Playing "time"

This is the basic swing pattern for Jazz Drumming (with and without bass drum). Practice each until they are "automatic".

Achieving Variety of the Ride Pattern

Although many drum parts are notated with a strictly repetitive ride cymbal pattern, in practice jazz drummers use a wide variety of cymbal rhythms. Practice each of the rhythms below so that you can execute them with steady time and good feel. When playing the exercises and songs in this book feel free to use any of the rhythmic patterns listed below.

1. 2. 3. 4.

5. 6. 7. 8.

Using the Bass Drum in the Swing Pattern

When playing the basic swing pattern the bass drum can play quarter notes on all four beats of the bar very softly or it can be omitted. It is important to develop a very light bass drum as it can easily sound heavy and cover up the notes of the bass line. It is often said that the bass drum should be "felt but not heard"..

Playing with the Ensemble (Playing "Figures")

In jazz the drummer does more than just play the beat pattern of the song (often called "playing time"). Good jazz drummers usually adjust their playing to fit the melodies and rhythms that the ensemble plays. These melodies and rhythms are called "figures."

There are two basic types of figures:

1. Ensemble "figures" played by the entire band
2. Section "figures" played by one section

Figures may be interpreted in a variety of ways. Ensemble figures can be reinforced with snare, bass drum, toms, and cymbals, while section figures are most often reinforced lightly while the ride cymbal and hi-hat continue to play the basic beat pattern of the music. It is important that the drum part enhance and not detract from the overall effect of the music.

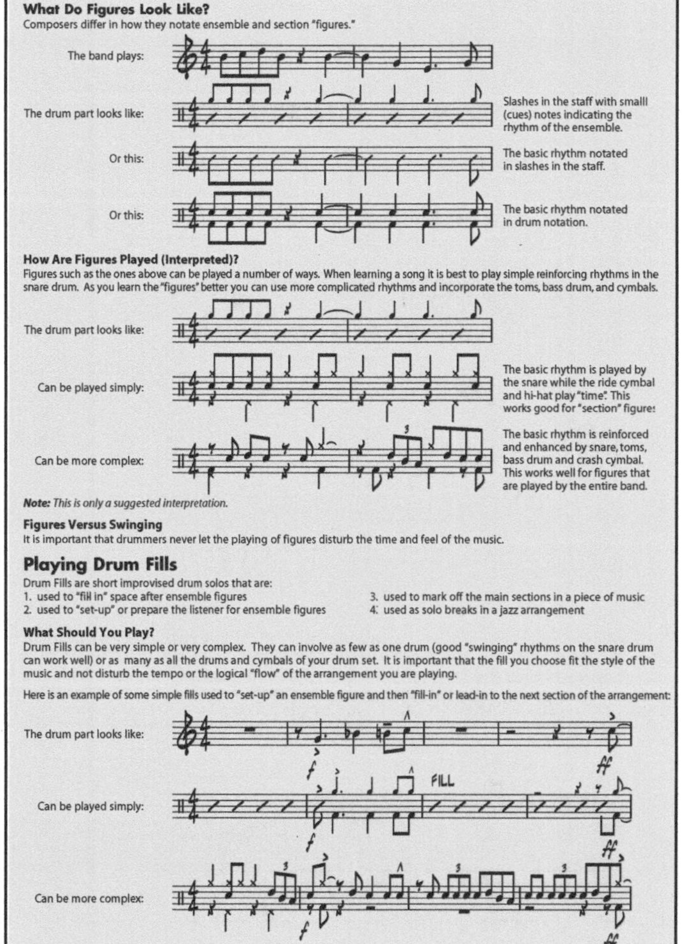

What Do Figures Look Like?

Composers differ in how they notate ensemble and section "figures."

The band plays:

The drum part looks like: Slashes in the staff with smalll (cues) notes indicating the rhythm of the ensemble.

Or this: The basic rhythm notated in slashes in the staff.

Or this: The basic rhythm notated in drum notation.

How Are Figures Played (Interpreted)?

Figures such as the ones above can be played a number of ways. When learning a song it is best to play simple reinforcing rhythms in the snare drum. As you learn the "figures" better you can use more complicated rhythms and incorporate the toms, bass drum, and cymbals.

The drum part looks like:

Can be played simply: The basic rhythm is played by the snare while the ride cymbal and hi-hat play "time". This works good for "section" figures

Can be more complex: The basic rhythm is reinforced and enhanced by snare, toms, bass drum and crash cymbal. This works well for figures that are played by the entire band.

Note: *This is only a suggested interpretation.*

Figures Versus Swinging

It is important that drummers never let the playing of figures disturb the time and feel of the music.

Playing Drum Fills

Drum Fills are short improvised drum solos that are:

1. used to "fill in" space after ensemble figures
2. used to "set-up" or prepare the listener for ensemble figures
3. used to mark off the main sections in a piece of music
4. used as solo breaks in a jazz arrangement

What Should You Play?

Drum Fills can be very simple or very complex. They can involve as few as one drum (good "swinging" rhythms on the snare drum can work well) or as many as all the drums and cymbals of your drum set. It is important that the fill you choose fit the style of the music and not disturb the tempo or the logical "flow" of the arrangement you are playing.

Here is an example of some simple fills used to "set-up" an ensemble figure and then "fill-in" or lead-in to the next section of the arrangement:

The drum part looks like:

Can be played simply:

Can be more complex:

DAILY DRILLS, WARM-UPS AND WORKOUTS

1. BASIC SCALE AND STYLE WORKOUT #1 – Major Scale

2. BASIC SCALE AND STYLE WORKOUT #2 – Major Scale

SWING

LATIN ROCK (STRAIGHT 8THS)

ALTO SAX
BARITONE SAX

TENOR SAX

TRUMPET

TROMBONE

GUITAR

PIANO

BASS

DRUMS

C TREBLE/
VIBES

3. BASIC SCALE AND STYLE WORKOUT #3 – Mixolydian Mode

SWING

LATIN ROCK (STRAIGHT 8THS)

ALTO SAX
BARITONE SAX

TENOR SAX

TRUMPET

TROMBONE

GUITAR

PIANO

BASS

DRUMS

C TREBLE/
VIBES

4. BASIC SCALE AND STYLE WORKOUT #4 – Mixolydian Mode

5. BASIC SCALE AND STYLE WORKOUT #5 – Dorian Mode

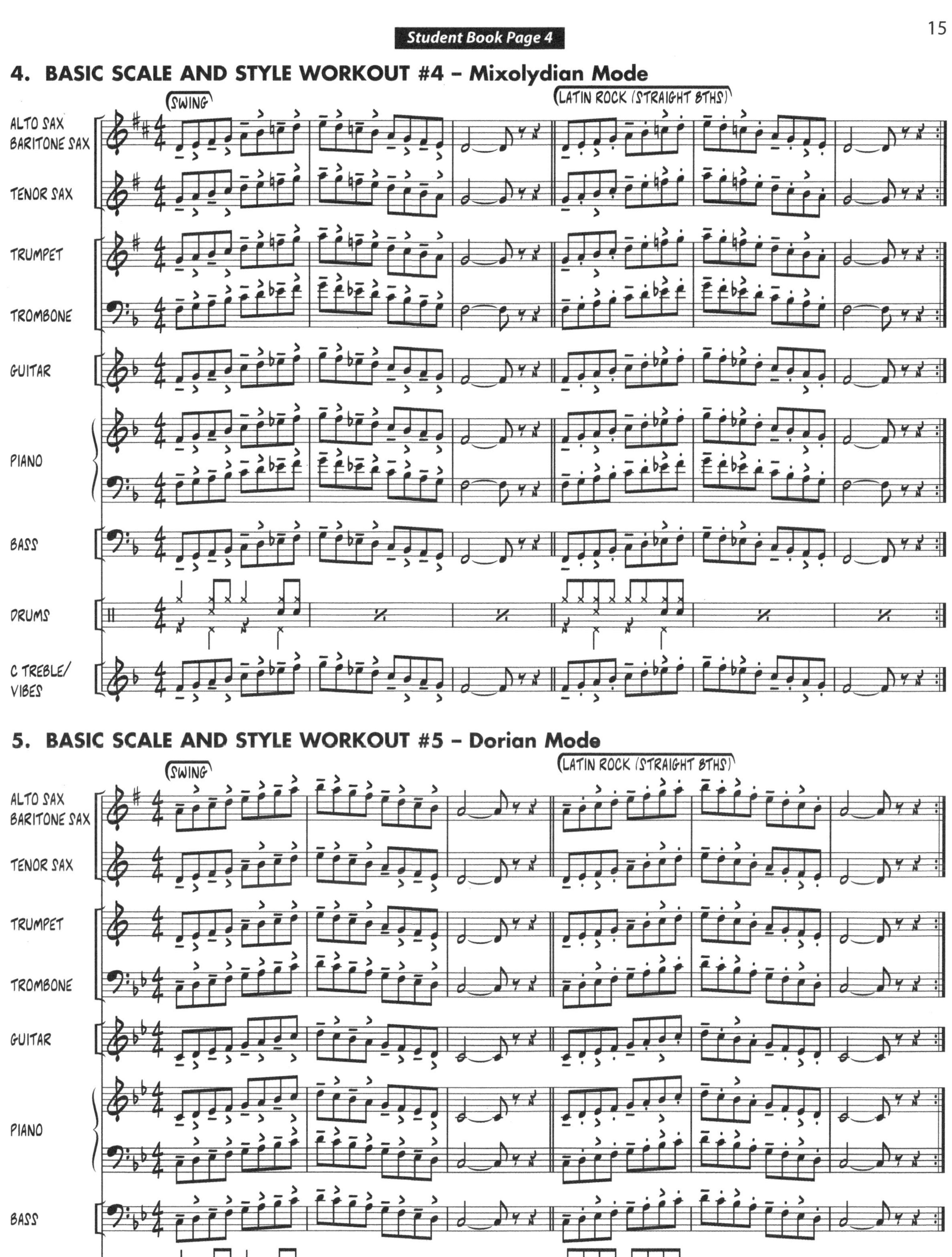

6. BASIC SCALE AND STYLE WORKOUT #6 – Harmonic Minor

RHYTHM WORKOUTS FOR READING AND STYLE

7. HALF MEASURE RHYTHMS

A. SAX
B. SAX
Doo Doo Dot
Dot
Doo Dot
Bah Doo Dot
Bah Dot
T. SAX
TPT.
TBN.
GTR.
PNO.
BASS
DMS.
C/VIB.
A. SAX
B. SAX
Bah
Dot
Doo Dot
Dot
Dot
T. SAX
TPT.
TBN.
GTR.
PNO.
BASS
DMS.
C/VIB.

8. COMBINING COMMON RHYTHMS #1

9. COMBINING COMMON RHYTHMS #2

10. COMBINING COMMON RHYTHMS #3

11. COMBINING COMMON RHYTHMS #4

12. COMBINING COMMON RHYTHMS #5

13. COMBINING COMMON RHYTHMS #6 – Adding Ties

RHYTHM WORKOUTS FOR READING AND STYLE (STRAIGHT 8THS)

14. COMBINING COMMON RHYTHMS #7

A. SAX
B. SAX
T. SAX
TPT.
TBN.
GTR.
PNO.
BASS
DMS.
C/VIB.

15. COMBINING COMMON RHYTHMS #8

(STRAIGHT 8THS)

ALTO SAX
BARITONE SAX
TENOR SAX
TRUMPET
TROMBONE
GUITAR
PIANO
BASS
DRUMS
C TREBLE/
VIBES

Student Book Page 6

16. SCALE AND RHYTHM WORKOUT

Student Book Page 6

17. MELODY AND RHYTHM WORKOUT #1

18. MELODY AND RHYTHM WORKOUT #2

Student Book Page 7

JAZZ EXPRESSION WORKOUTS

19. STYLE CONCEPT – Syllables for Jazz Expression

20. SCOOPS, FALLS, BENDS AND DOITS

21. PLOPS, GLISSANDI AND FLIPS

22. MELODY AND EXPRESSION WORKOUT #1

23. MELODY AND RHYTHM WORKOUT #2

24. NEW CONCEPT: GHOSTED NOTES

Often single notes in jazz lines are played very softly and without accent. These notes can be notated with an "x" instead of a notehead. Lines with ghosted 8th notes are usually played legato.

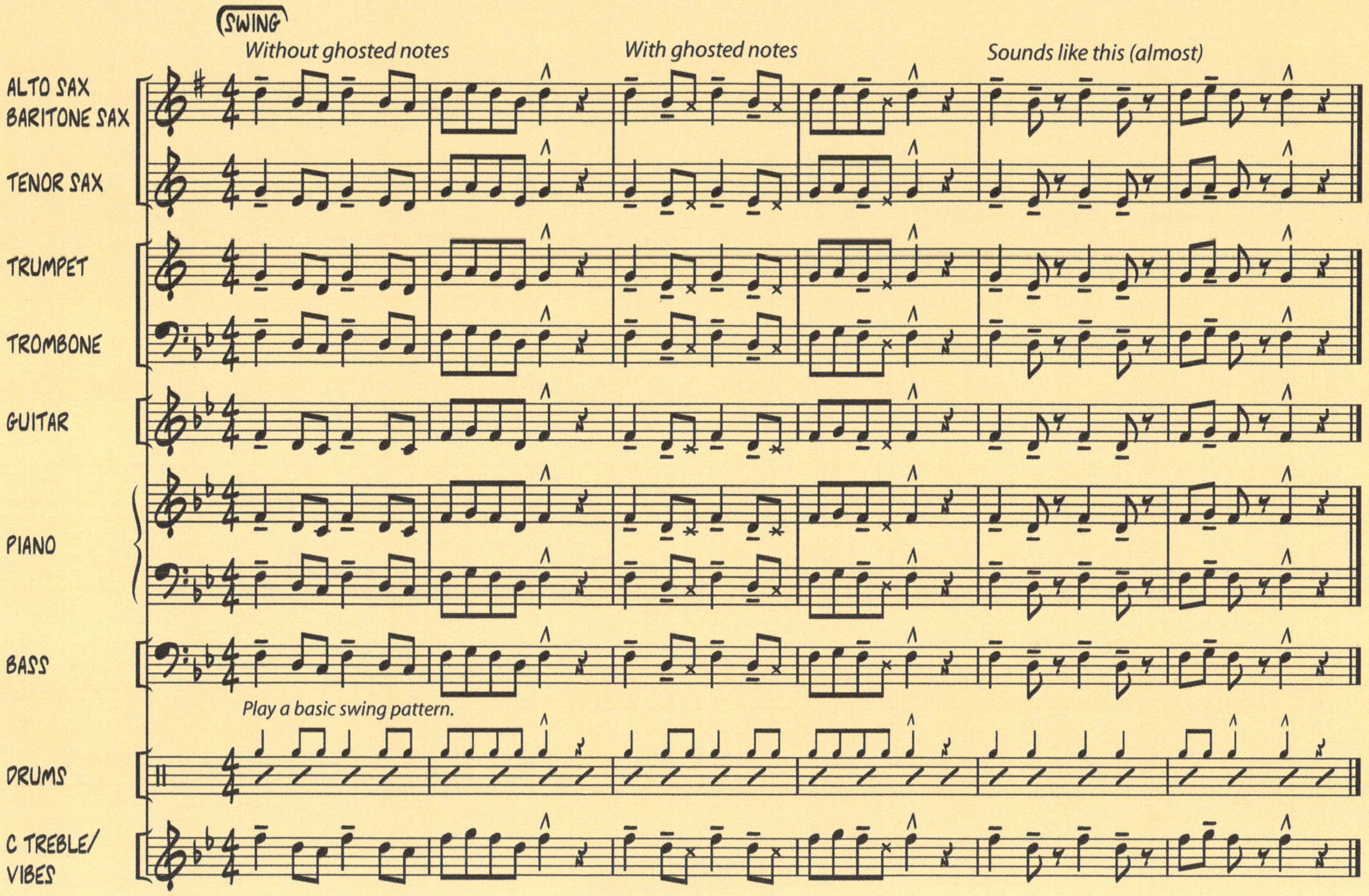

SWING

Without ghosted notes *With ghosted notes* *Sounds like this (almost)*

ALTO SAX
BARITONE SAX

TENOR SAX

TRUMPET

TROMBONE

GUITAR

PIANO

BASS

Play a basic swing pattern.

DRUMS

C TREBLE/
VIBES

25. JAZZ EXPRESSION ETUDE

SWING

ALTO SAX
BARITONE SAX

TENOR SAX

TRUMPET

TROMBONE

GUITAR

PIANO

BASS

Play a basic swing pattern.

DRUMS

C TREBLE/
VIBES

Student Book Page 7

A. SAX
B. SAX

T. SAX

TPT.

TBN.

GTR.

PNO.

BASS

DMS.

C/VIB.

Drums Only

Playing With Brushes

Brushes are used to produce a smooth pulse at softer volumes. There many different approaches to brush playing. Often in Latin and country music brushes are used as if they are regular drumsticks. In jazz performed at slow and medium tempos brush playing uses the same technique and grip as stick playing with one difference: at least one of the brushes (usually the left) maintains direct contact with the drum head at all times. The diagrams below shows a basic brush pattern in 4/4 swing time and a common variation.

Basic Brush Pattern in 4/4 Swing

The Right Brush plays the basic swing cymbal pattern by tapping back and forth The brush is lifted between beats.

The Left Brush makes a clockwise circle on the drumhead every two beats. If consistent contact is maintained the sound will be a steady "swish" and the hands will seem to cross on beats 2 and 4. For slower tempos each circle can last one beat.

Variation:

Both hands move in opposite directions in a circular motion (one hand clockwise and the other counter-clockwise). To get the "feel" for this technique, practice making circles in time with both hands producing a steady "swishing" sound.

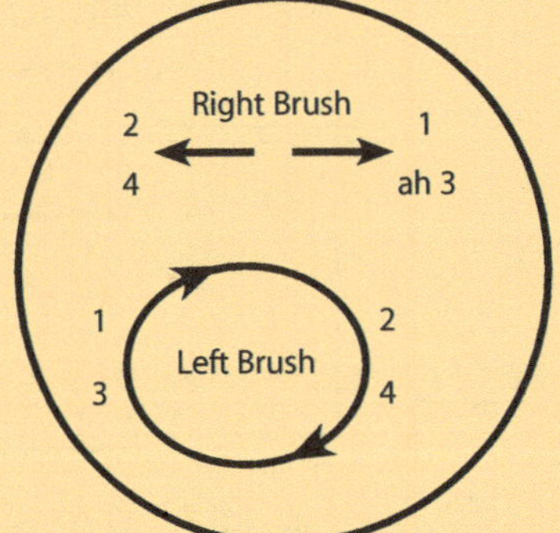

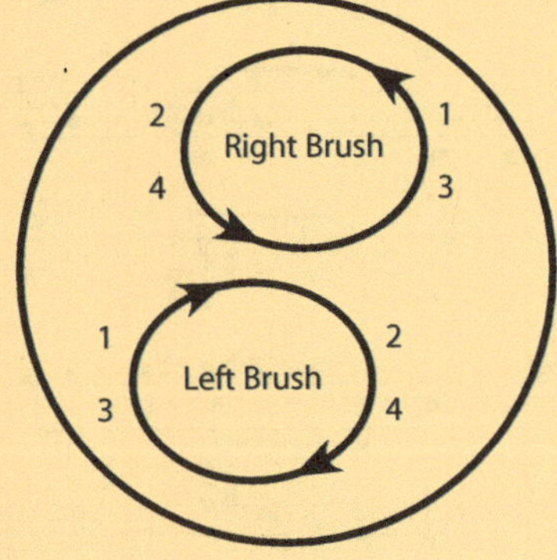

Hints:

- Accents can be achieved by lifting the brush and tapping the drum head or by sweeping with a bit more weight.
- Some techniques combine the "swishing" sweep with a lifting and tapping motion in one of the hands.
- Generally only the tip of the brush is used for softer volumes. For louder volumes or more aggressive accents two or three inches of the brush can strike the drum head.

Playing the brushes in 3/4 time requires that the beat pattern (in the "tapping" hand) be adjusted to:

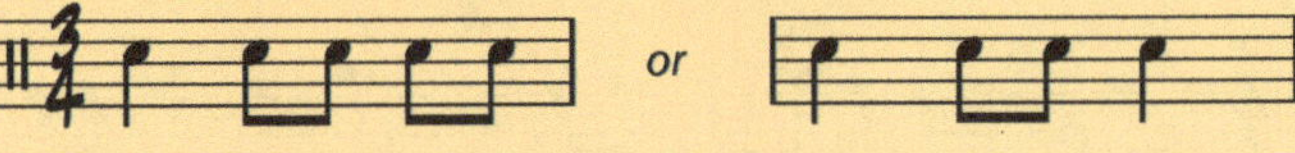

WARM-UPS FOR BALANCE BLEND AND INTONATION

26. BALANCE AND BLEND WORKOUT (Concert B♭ Major)

27. BALANCE AND BLEND WORKOUT (Concert F Major)

28. BALANCE AND BLEND WORKOUT (Concert B♭ Mixolydian)

29. BALANCE AND BLEND WORKOUT (Concert F Mixolydian)

30. BALANCE AND BLEND WORKOUT (Concert E♭ Mixolydian)

31. BALANCE AND BLEND WORKOUT (Concert C Mixolydian)

32. BALANCE AND BLEND WORKOUT (Concert C Dorian)

Student Book Page 9

MAJOR SCALES BY NUMBERS

33. MAJOR SCALE WORKOUT

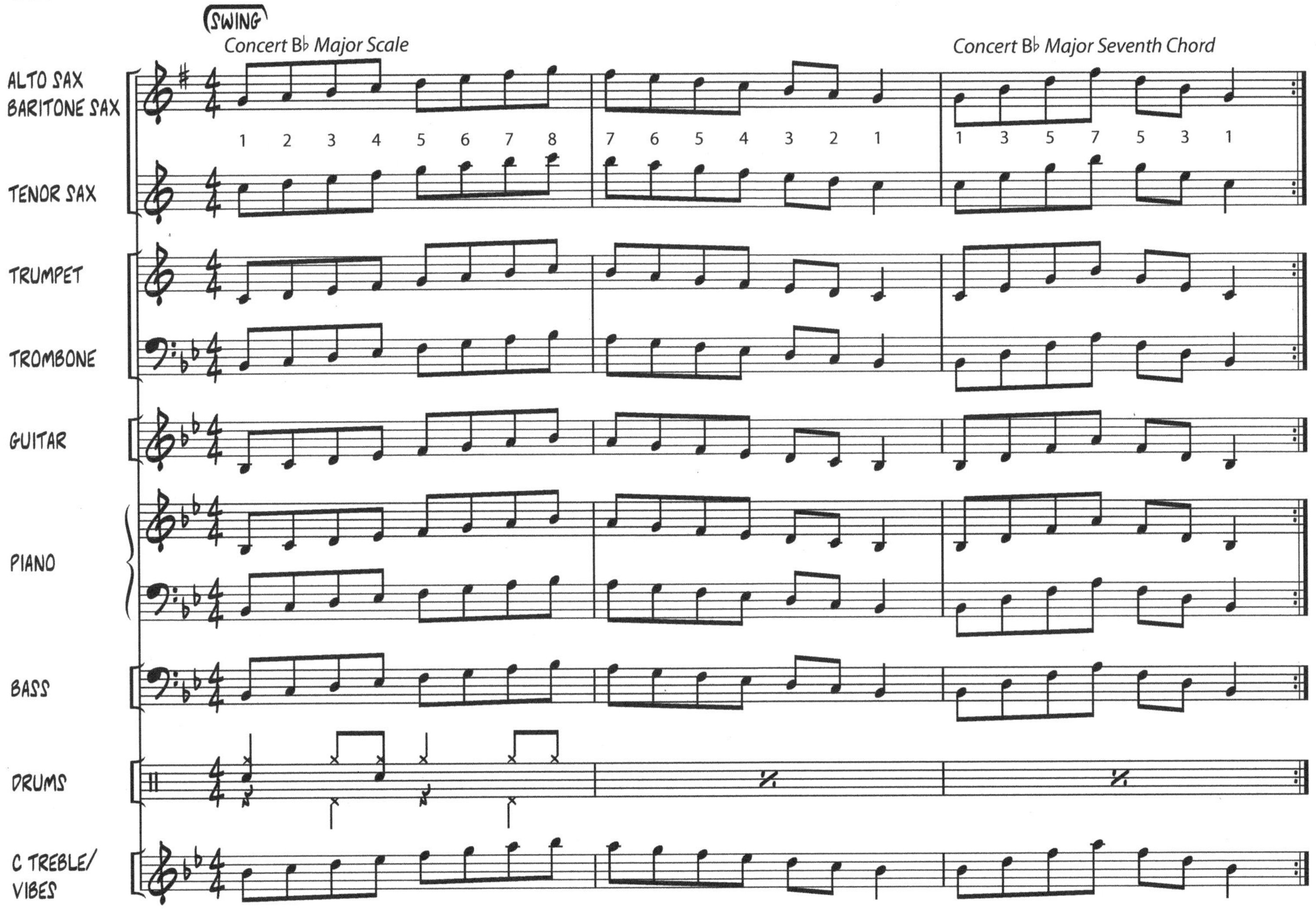

SWING
Concert B♭ Major Scale
Concert B♭ Major Seventh Chord
ALTO SAX
BARITONE SAX
1 2 3 4 5 6 7 8
7 6 5 4 3 2 1
1 3 5 7 5 3 1
TENOR SAX
TRUMPET
TROMBONE
GUITAR
PIANO
BASS
DRUMS
C TREBLE/
VIBES

34. MAJOR SCALE BY THE NUMBERS #1 *Play using only the numbers.*

SWING
Concert B♭ Major Scale
Concert B♭ Major Seventh Chord
SXS./TPTS./
TBNS./RHYTHM
1 2 3 4 5 6 7 8
7 6 5 4 3 2 1
1 3 5 7 5 3 1
DRUMS

35. MAJOR SCALE BY THE NUMBERS #2

SWING
SXS./TPTS./
TBNS./RHYTHM
1 2 3 4 5
5 4 3 2 1
1 2 3 4 5 4 3 2
1
1 2 3 5 4 3 2 7
below "1"
1
DRUMS
4

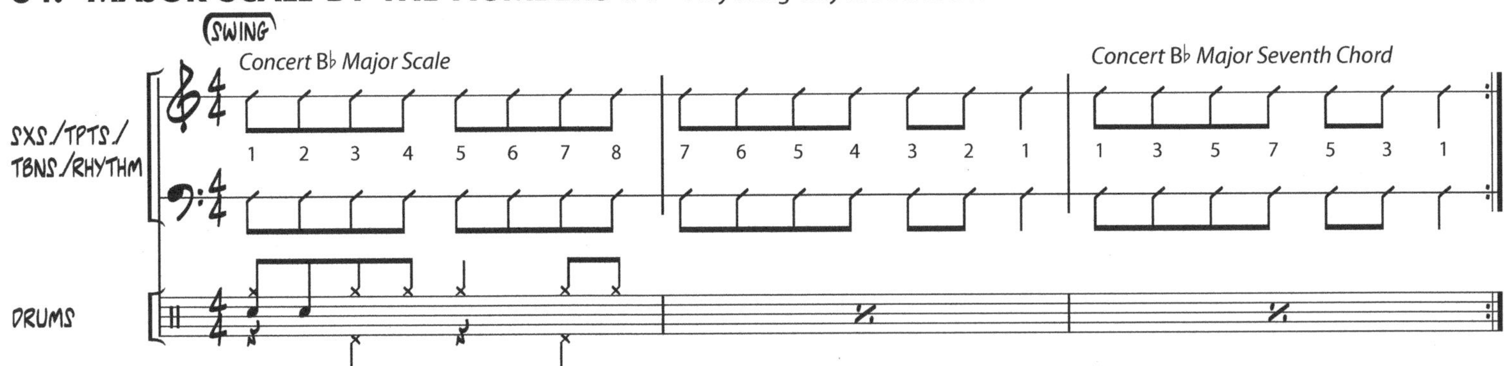

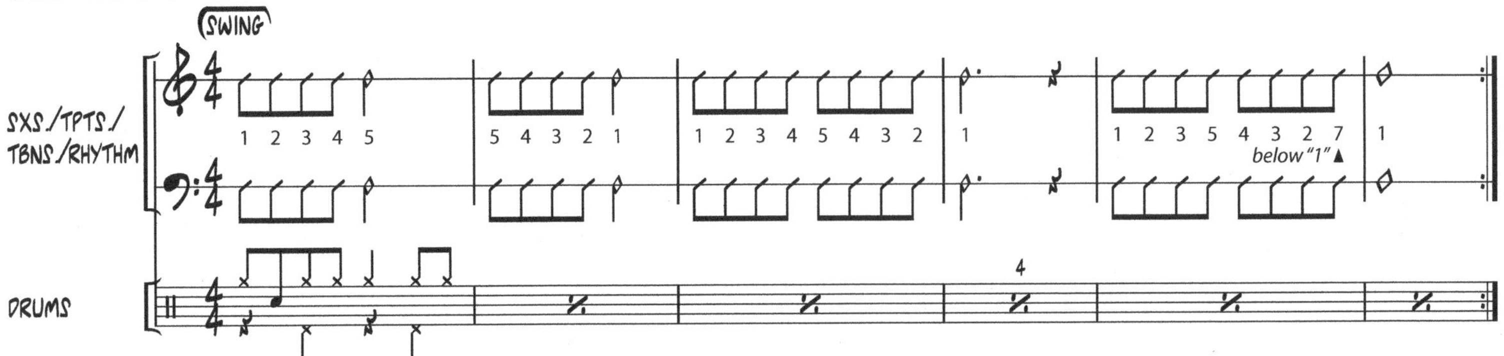

36. MAJOR SCALE BY THE NUMBERS #3

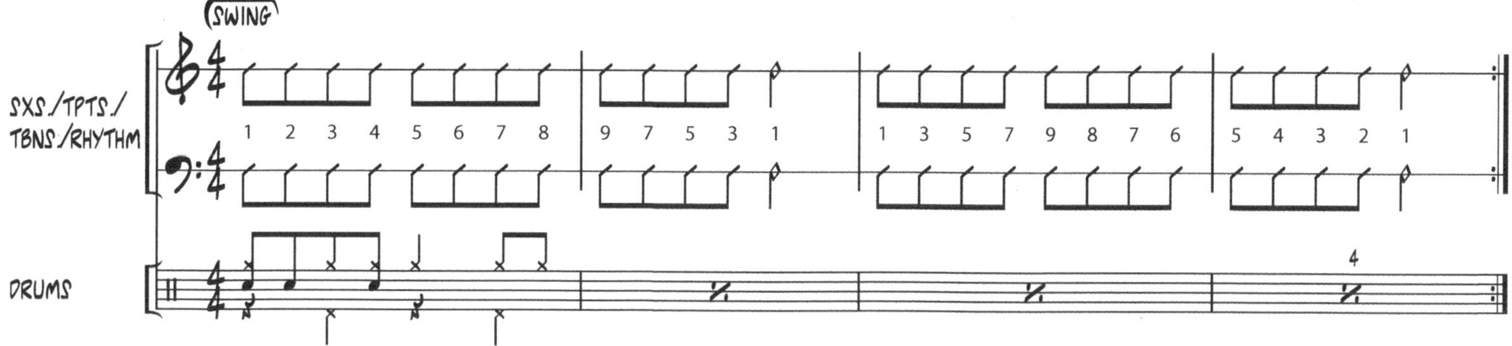

37. MAJOR SCALE BY THE NUMBERS #4

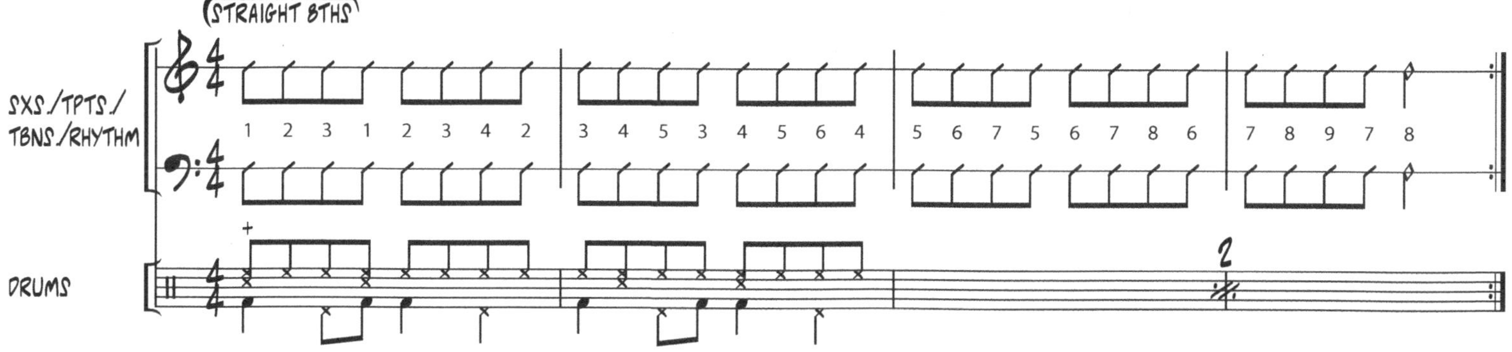

38. MAJOR SCALE BY THE NUMBERS #5

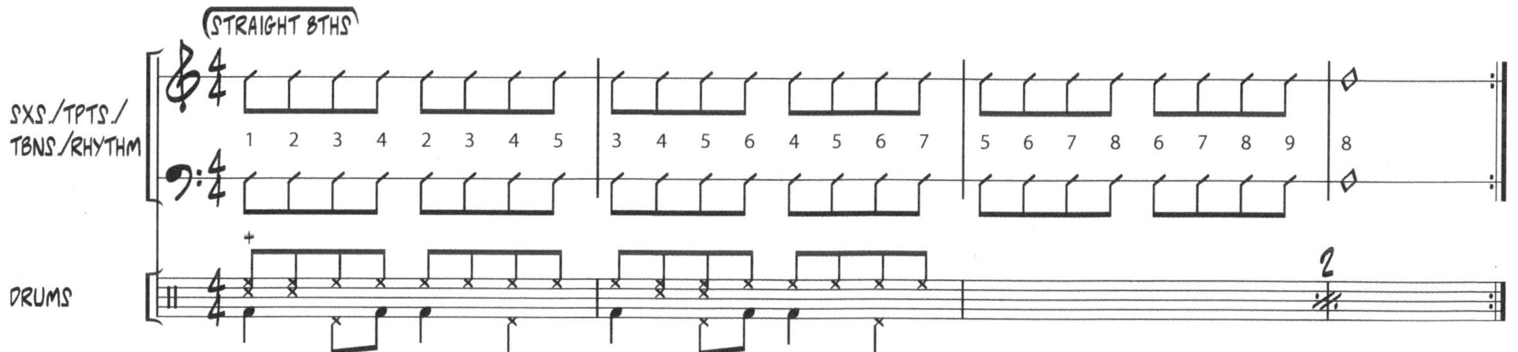

39. MAJOR SCALE BY THE NUMBERS #6

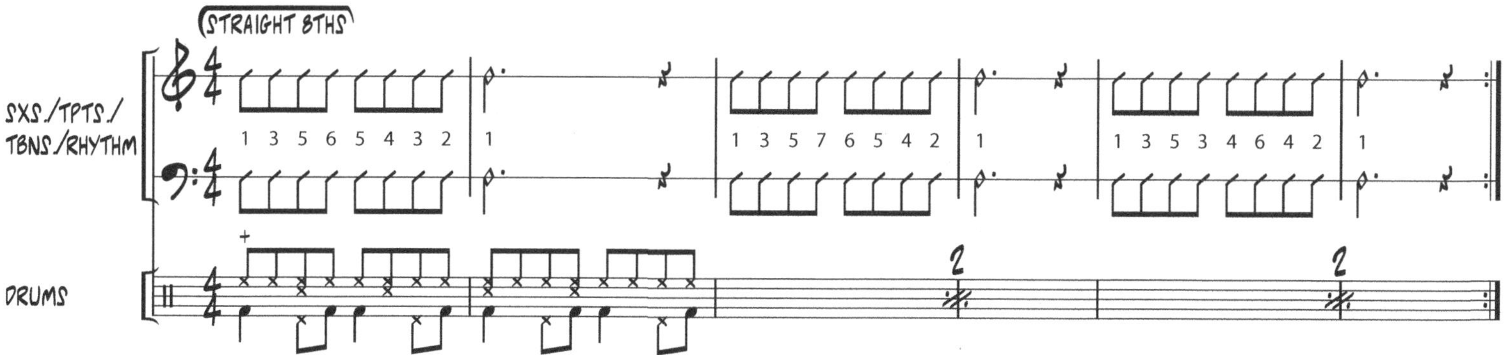

Additional Workouts – Repeat the scale patterns in exercises 34 through 39 using these common keys.

F Major Scale — *E♭ Major Scale*

ALTO SAX / BARITONE SAX — 1 2 3 4 5 6 7 8 7 6 5 4 3 2 1 — 1 2 3 4 5 6 7 8 7 6 5 4 3 2 1

TENOR SAX

TRUMPET

TROMBONE

GUITAR

PIANO

BASS

DRUMS

C TREBLE/ VIBES

MIXOLYDIAN MODE BY NUMBERS

40. MIXOLYDIAN WORKOUT

SWING

Concert B♭ Mixolydian Mode — *Concert B♭ Dominant Seventh Chord*

ALTO SAX / BARITONE SAX — 1 2 3 4 5 6 ♭7 8 — ♭7 6 5 4 3 2 1 — 1 3 5 ♭7 5 3 1

TENOR SAX

TRUMPET

TROMBONE

GUITAR

PIANO

BASS

DRUMS

C TREBLE/ VIBES

41. MIXOLYDIAN BY THE NUMBERS #1 *Play using the numbers.*

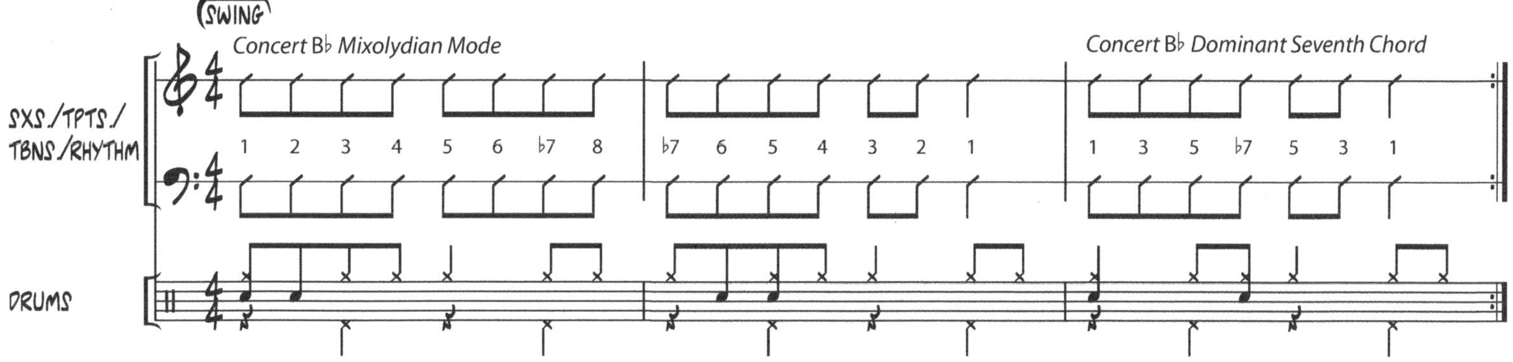

42. MIXOLYDIAN BY THE NUMBERS #2

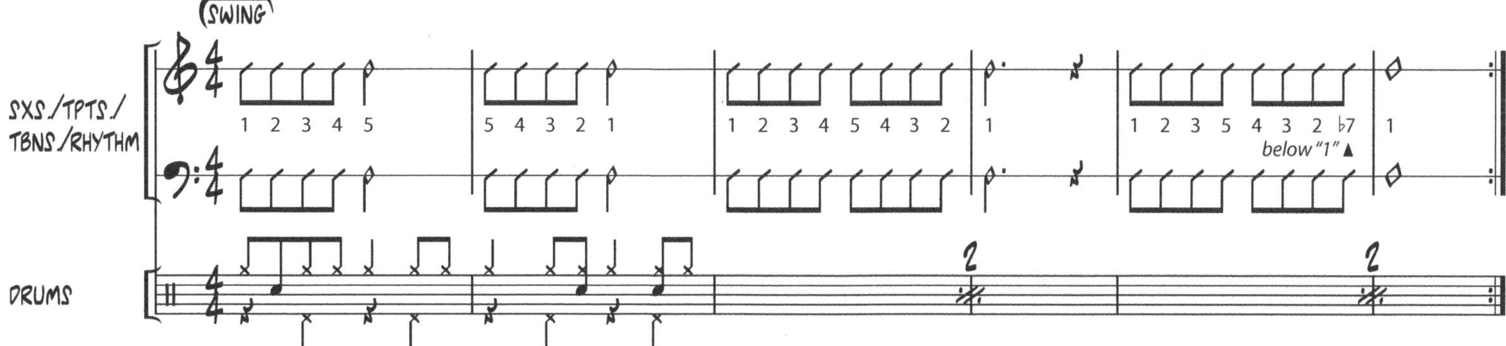

43. MIXOLYDIAN BY THE NUMBERS #3

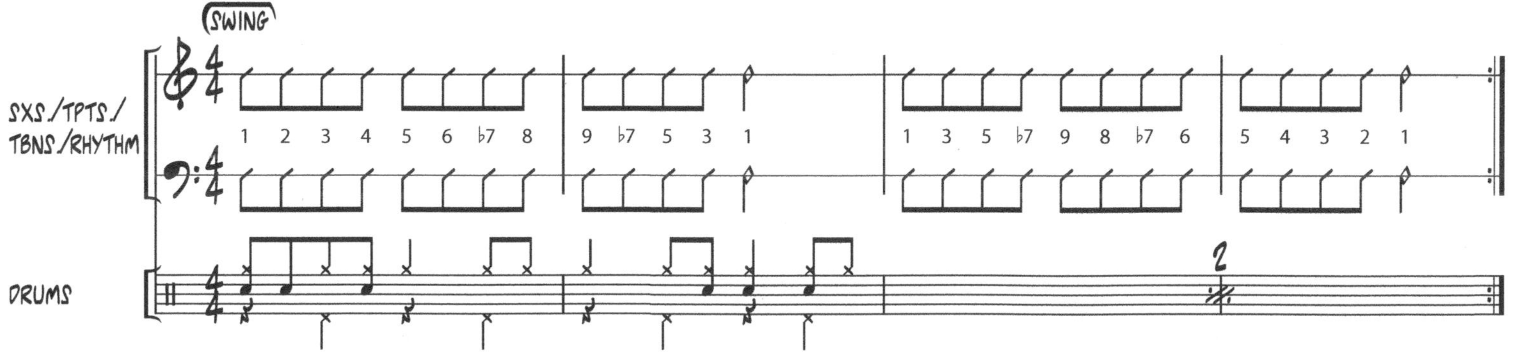

44. MIXOLYDIAN BY THE NUMBERS #4

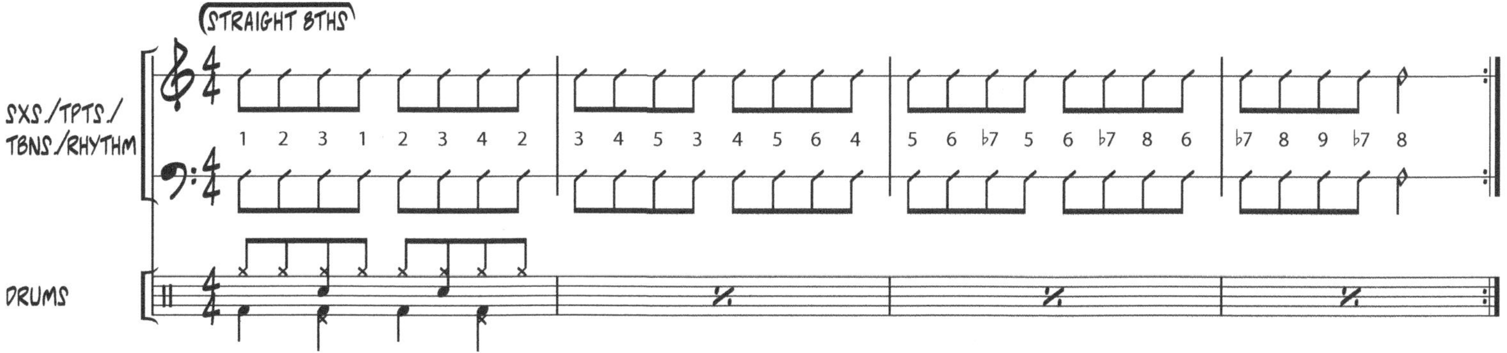

45. MIXOLYDIAN BY THE NUMBERS #5

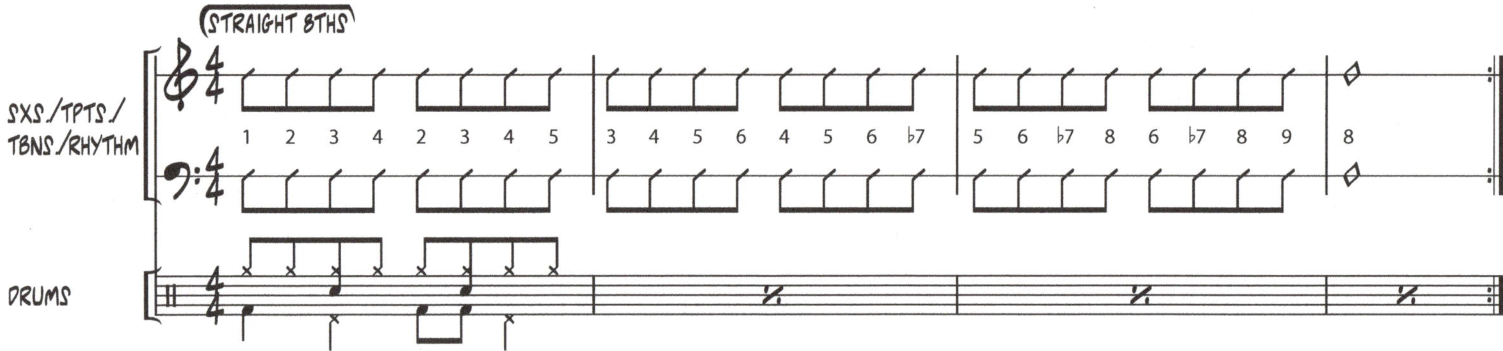

46. MIXOLYDIAN BY THE NUMBERS #6

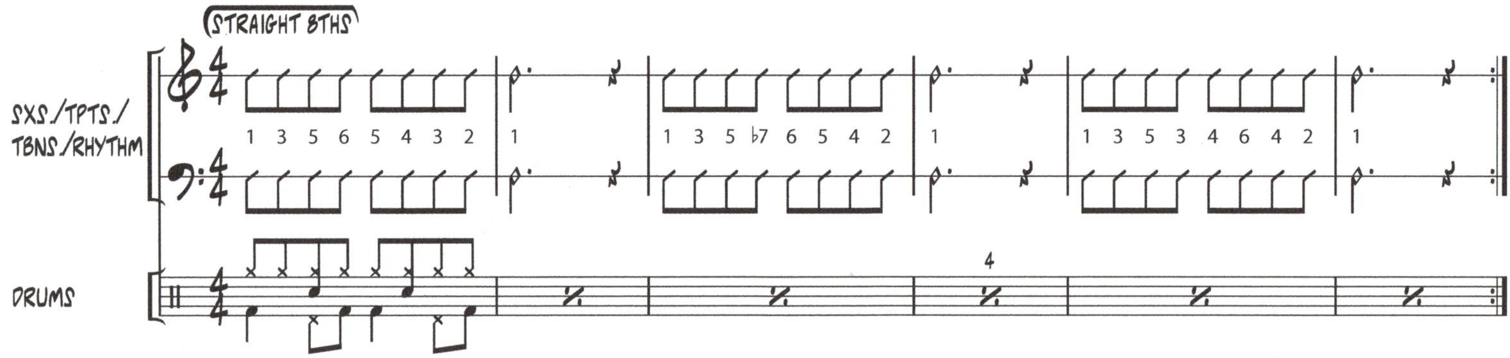

Additional Workouts – Repeat the scale patterns in exercises 40 through 46 using these common Mixolydian modes.

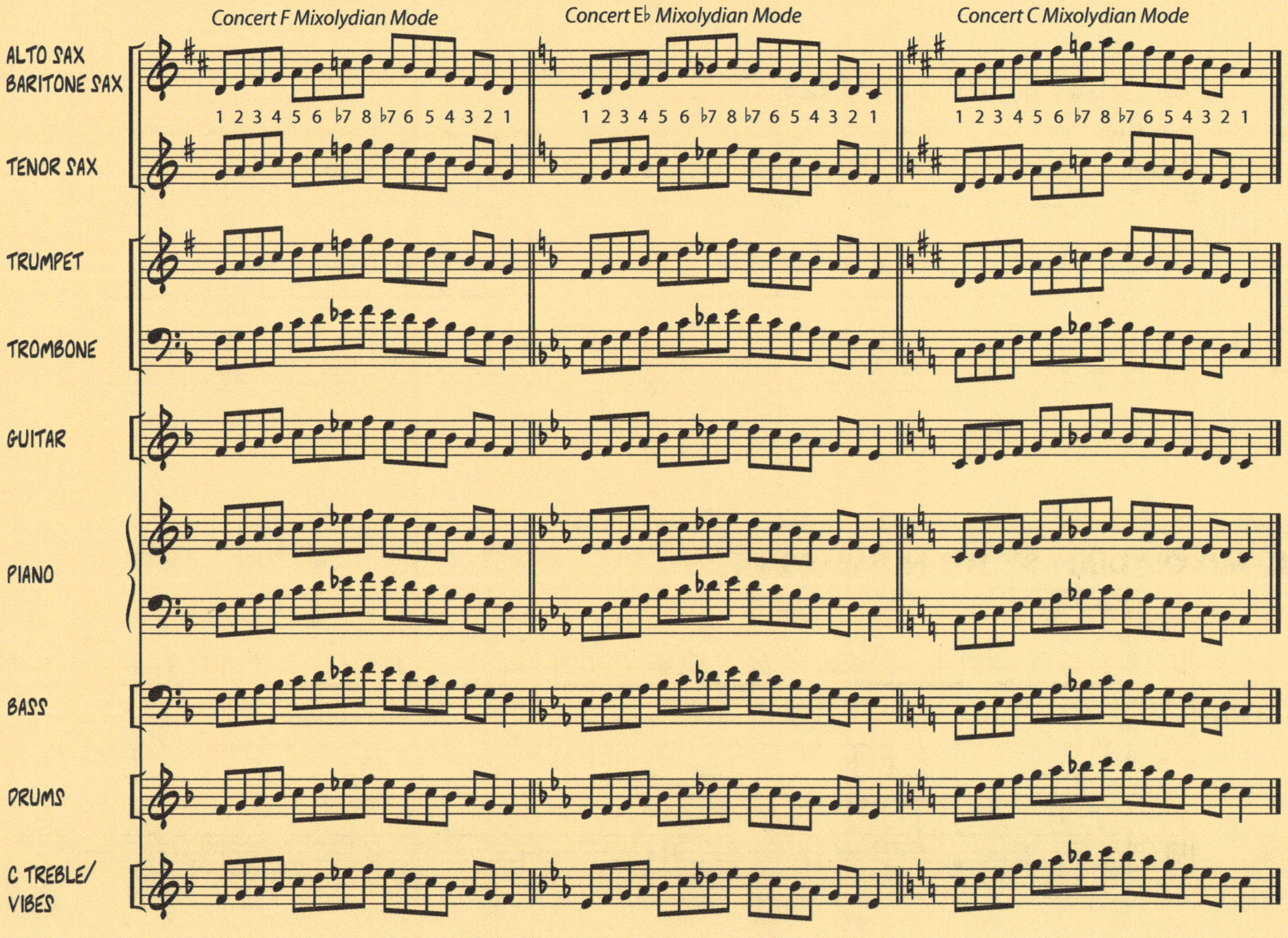

Concert F Mixolydian Mode *Concert E♭ Mixolydian Mode* *Concert C Mixolydian Mode*

ALTO SAX
BARITONE SAX

1 2 3 4 5 6 ♭7 8 ♭7 6 5 4 3 2 1 1 2 3 4 5 6 ♭7 8 ♭7 6 5 4 3 2 1 1 2 3 4 5 6 ♭7 8 ♭7 6 5 4 3 2 1

TENOR SAX

TRUMPET

TROMBONE

GUITAR

PIANO

BASS

DRUMS

C TREBLE/
VIBES

DORIAN MODE BY NUMBERS

47. DORIAN WORKOUT

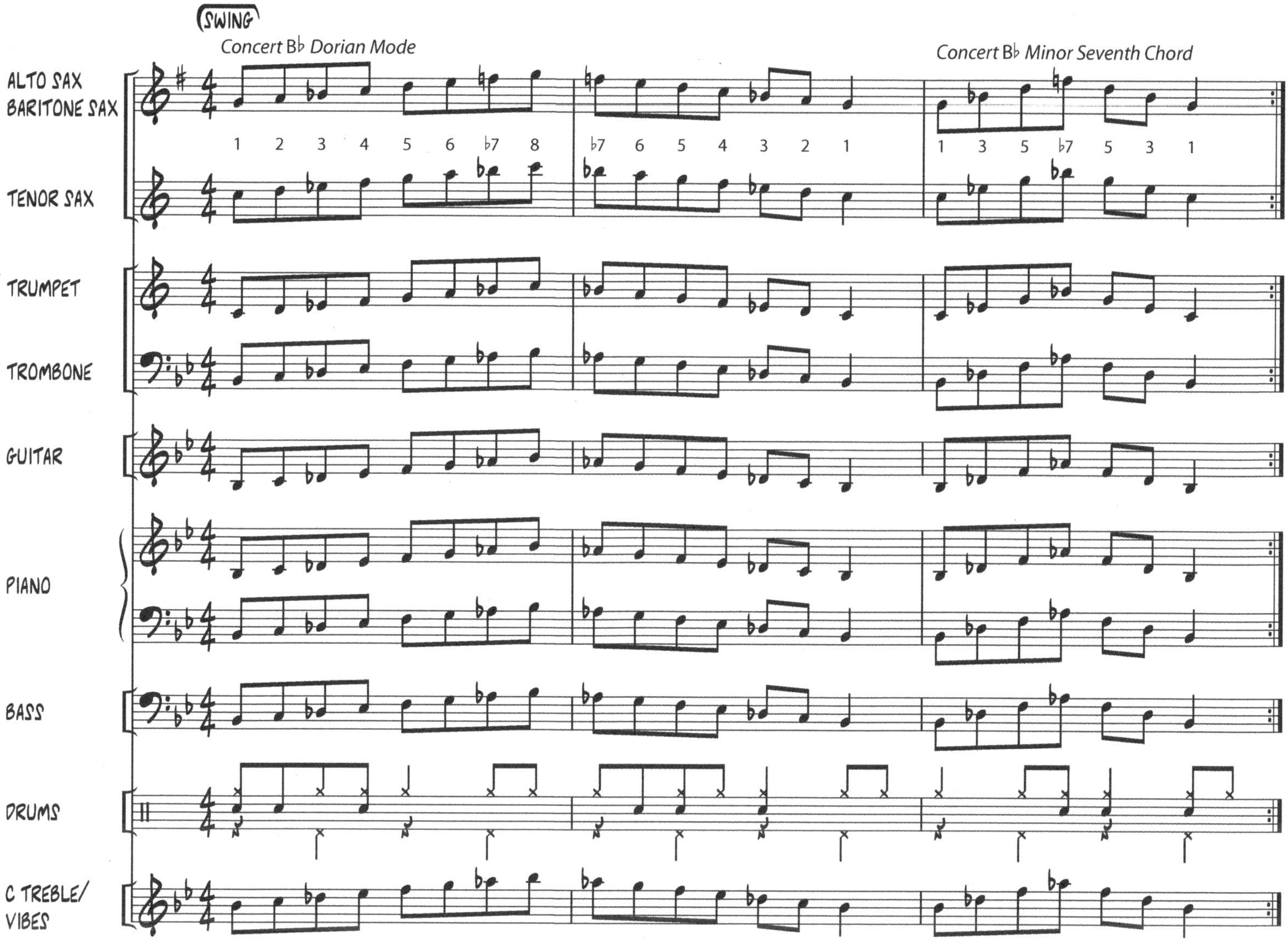

SWING
Concert B♭ Dorian Mode
Concert B♭ Minor Seventh Chord
ALTO SAX
BARITONE SAX
1 2 3 4 5 6 ♭7 8
♭7 6 5 4 3 2 1
1 3 5 ♭7 5 3 1
TENOR SAX
TRUMPET
TROMBONE
GUITAR
PIANO
BASS
DRUMS
C TREBLE/
VIBES

48. DORIAN BY THE NUMBERS #1 *Play using the numbers.*

SWING
Concert B♭ Dorian Mode
Concert B♭ Minor Seventh Chord
SXS./TPTS./
TBNS./RHYTHM
1 2 ♭3 4 5 6 ♭7 8
♭7 6 5 4 ♭3 2 1
1 ♭3 5 ♭7 5 ♭3 1
DRUMS

49. DORIAN BY THE NUMBERS #2

SWING
SXS./TPTS./
TBNS./RHYTHM
1 2 ♭3 4 5
5 4 ♭3 2 1
1 2 ♭3 4 5 4 ♭3 2
1
1 2 ♭3 5 4 ♭3 2 ♭7
below "1"▲
1
DRUMS
2
2

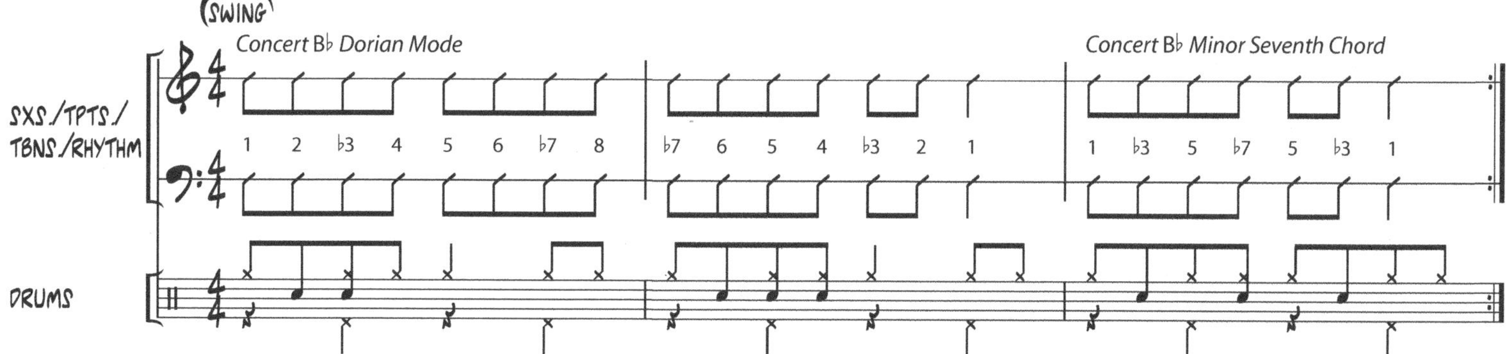

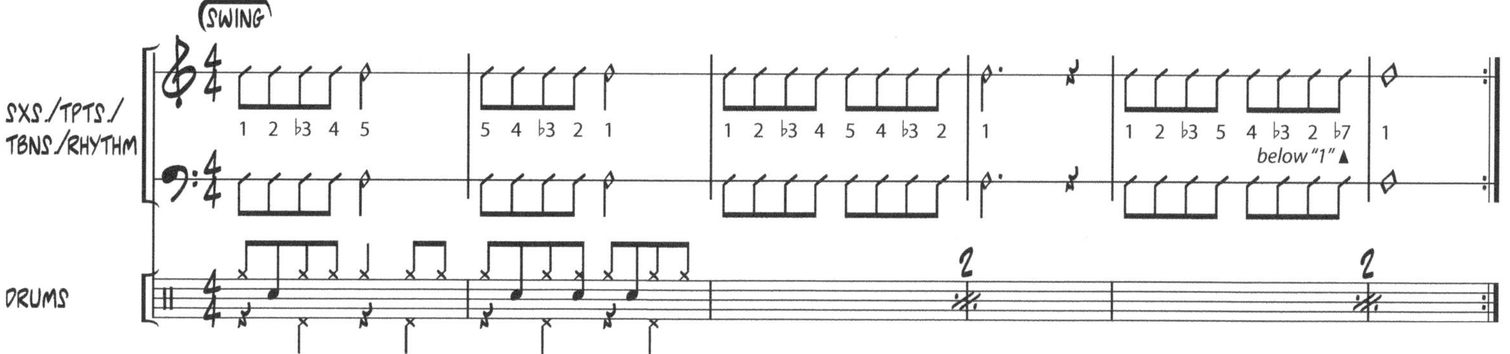

Student Book Page 11

50. DORIAN BY THE NUMBERS #3

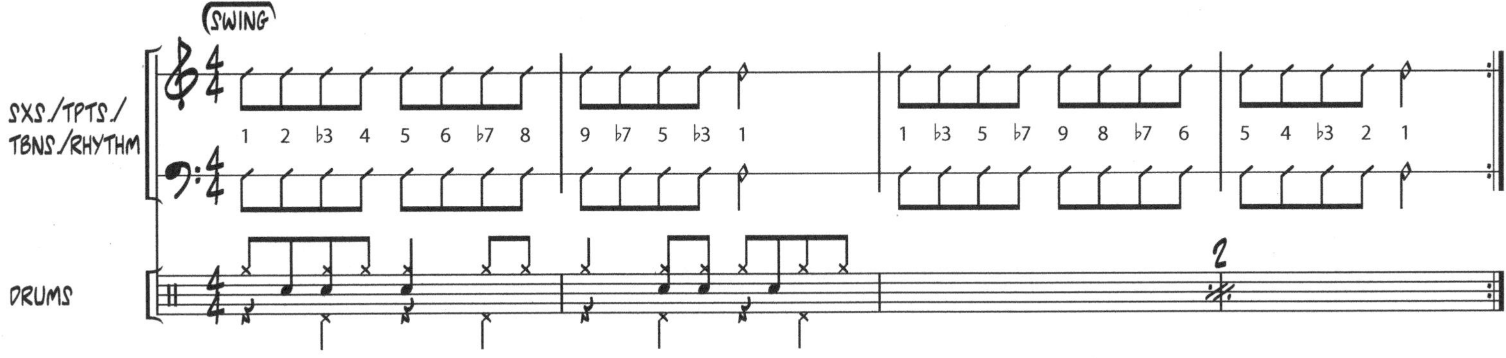

51. DORIAN BY THE NUMBERS #4

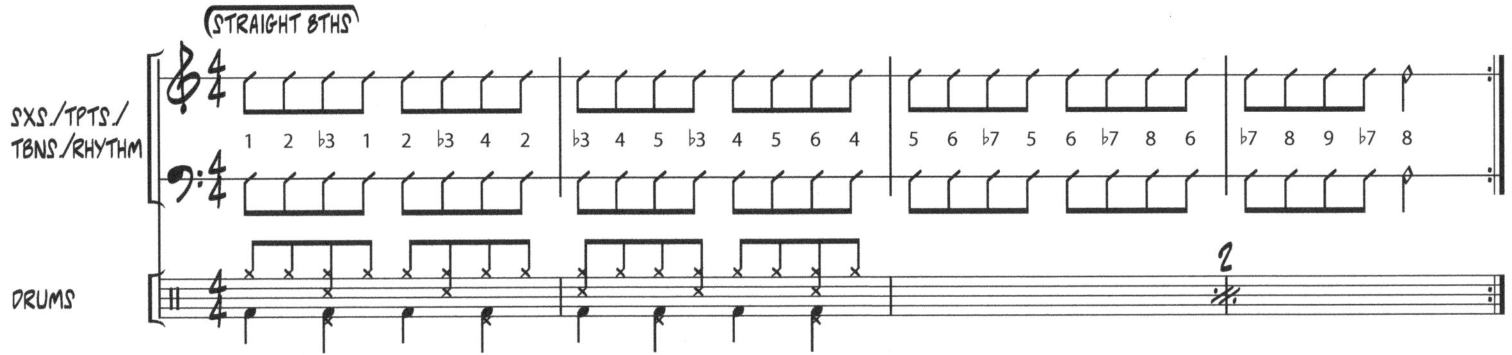

52. DORIAN BY THE NUMBERS #5

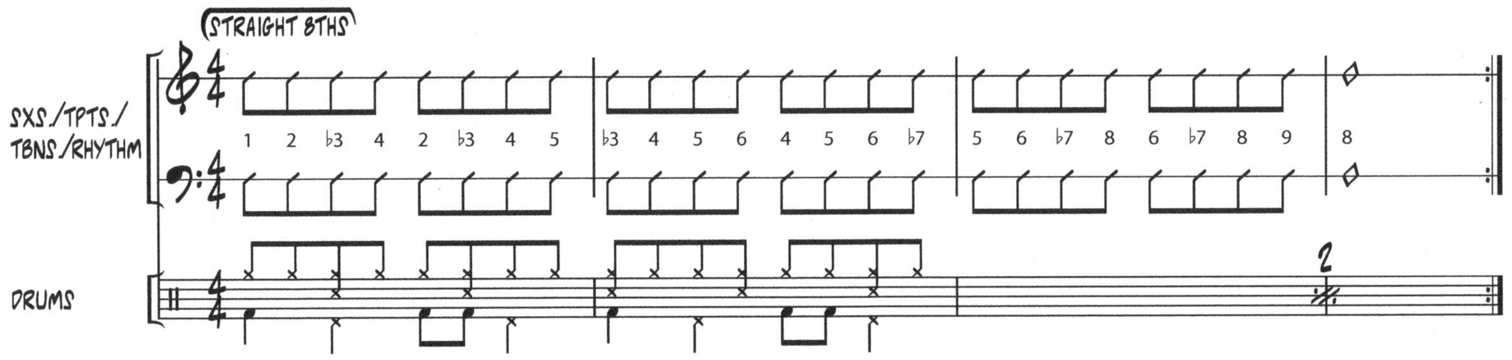

53. DORIAN BY THE NUMBERS #6

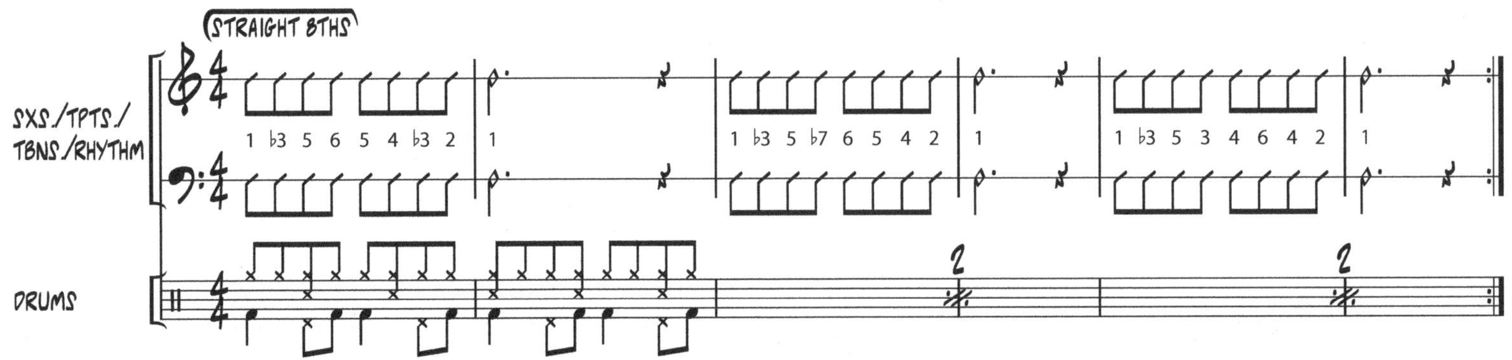

Additional Workouts – Repeat the scale patterns in exercises 47 through 53 using these common Dorian modes.

Concert F Dorian Mode · *Concert E♭ Dorian Mode* · *Concert C Dorian Mode*

ALTO SAX
BARITONE SAX

1 2 3 4 5 6 ♭7 8 ♭7 6 5 4 3 2 1 · 1 2 3 4 5 6 ♭7 8 ♭7 6 5 4 3 2 1 · 1 2 3 4 5 6 ♭7 8 ♭7 6 5 4 3 2 1

TENOR SAX

TRUMPET

TROMBONE

GUITAR

PIANO

BASS

DRUMS

C TREBLE/
VIBES

SCALE WORKOUTS – PENTATONIC AND BLUES SCALES IN CONCERT B♭

54. SCALE WORKOUT #1 – Minor Pentatonic

(STRAIGHT 8THS)

ALTO SAX
BARITONE SAX

1 ♭3 4 5 ♭7 5 4 ♭3 · 1 · 1 ♭3 4 5 ♭7 8 ♭7 5 · 4 ♭3 1 · 1 ♭3 4 5 ♭7 8 ♭3 1 · ♭7 5 4 ♭3 1

TENOR SAX

TRUMPET

TROMBONE

GUITAR

PIANO

BASS

DRUMS

C TREBLE/
VIBES

55. SCALE WORKOUT #2 – Minor Pentatonic

56. SCALE WORKOUT #3 – Minor Blues

57. SCALE WORKOUT #4 – Minor Blues

58. SCALE WORKOUT #5 – Major Blues

59. SCALE WORKOUT #6 – Major Blues

SCALE WORKOUTS – PENTATONIC AND BLUES SCALES IN CONCERT F

60. SCALE WORKOUT #1 – Minor Pentatonic

(SWING)

ALTO SAX
BARITONE SAX

1 b3 4 5 b7 5 4 b3 | 1 | 1 b3 4 5 b7 8 b7 5 | 4 b3 1 | 1 b3 4 5 b7 8 b3 1 | b7 5 4 b3 1

TENOR SAX

TRUMPET

TROMBONE

GUITAR

PIANO

BASS

DRUMS

C TREBLE/
VIBES

61. SCALE WORKOUT #2 – Minor Pentatonic

(SWING)

ALTO SAX
BARITONE SAX

TENOR SAX

TRUMPET

TROMBONE

GUITAR

PIANO

BASS

DRUMS

C TREBLE/
VIBES

62. SCALE WORKOUT #3 – Minor Blues

63. SCALE WORKOUT #4 – Minor Blues

64. SCALE WORKOUT #5 – Major Blues

65. SCALE WORKOUT #6 – Major Blues

Student Book Page 14

ADVANCED WORKOUTS – PENTATONIC AND BLUES SCALES IN CONCERT B♭

66. ADVANCED WORKOUT #1 – Minor Pentatonic

67. ADVANCED WORKOUT #2 – Minor Pentatonic

68. ADVANCED WORKOUT #3 – Minor Blues

69. ADVANCED WORKOUT #4 – Major Blues

70. ADVANCED WORKOUT #5 – Blues Riffs

71. ADVANCED WORKOUT #6 – Blues Riffs

ADVANCED WORKOUTS – PENTATONIC AND BLUES SCALES IN CONCERT F

72. ADVANCED WORKOUT #1 – Minor Pentatonic

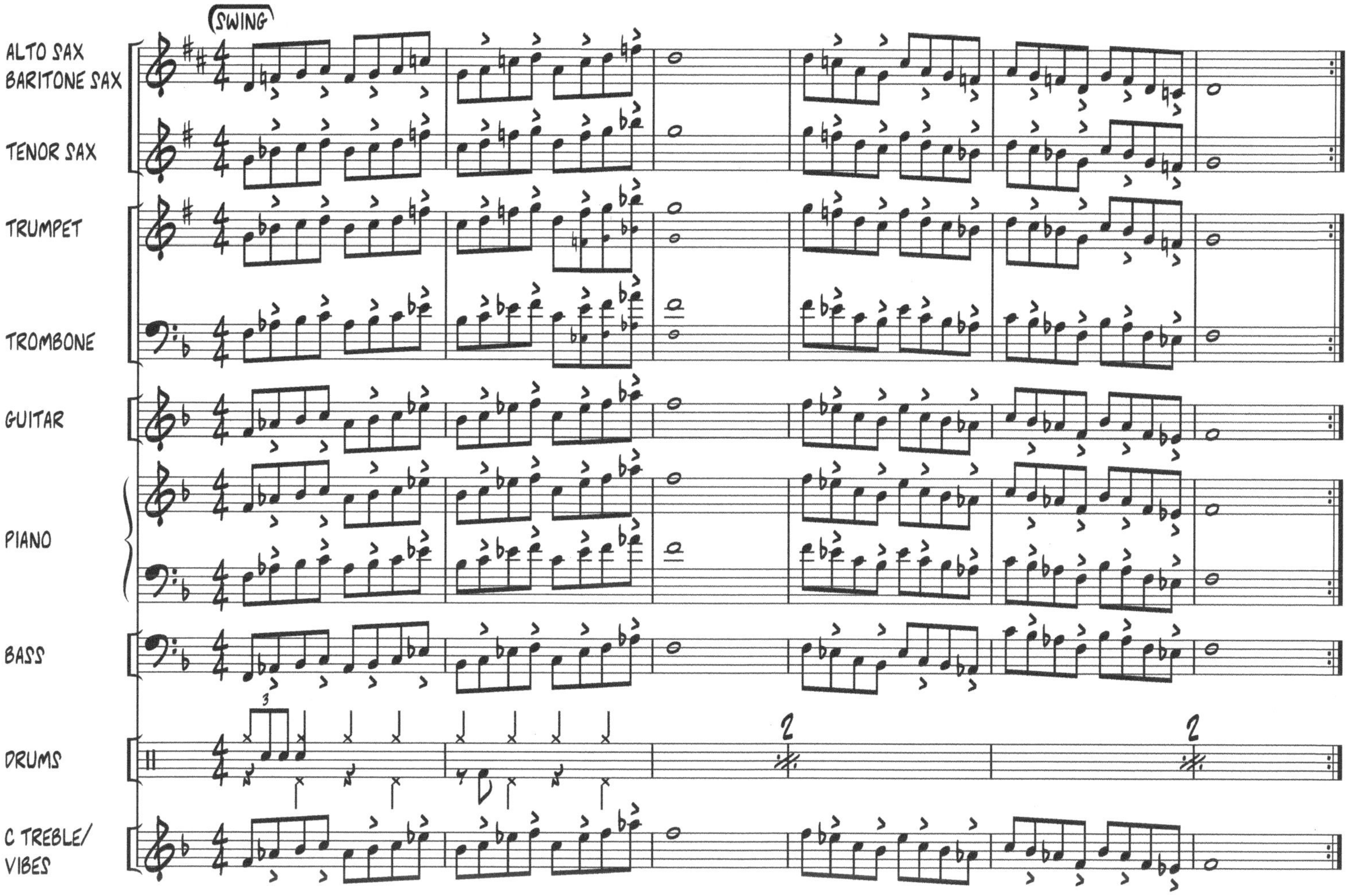

(SWING)

ALTO SAX
BARITONE SAX

TENOR SAX

TRUMPET

TROMBONE

GUITAR

PIANO

BASS

DRUMS

C TREBLE/
VIBES

73. ADVANCED WORKOUT #2 – Minor Pentatonic

(SWING)

ALTO SAX
BARITONE SAX

TENOR SAX

TRUMPET

TROMBONE

GUITAR

PIANO

BASS

DRUMS

C TREBLE/
VIBES

74. ADVANCED WORKOUT #3 – Minor Blues

75. ADVANCED WORKOUT #4 – Major Blues

76. ADVANCED WORKOUT #5 – Blues Riffs

77. ADVANCED WORKOUT #6 – Blues Riffs

LESSON #1 Reinventing Melody

Improvisation Concept – *Improvising by changing the rhythms of a melody (Reinvention).*

All Lesson #1 exercises are played in a Swing style.

78. SIMPLE MELODY *Start with a simple familiar melody.*

79. SYNCOPATION *Play notes early or late.*

80. ITERATION *Fill up long notes with rhythm.*

81. DISPLACEMENT *Move melody around.*

82. AUGMENTATION AND DIMINUTION

Make notes longer or shorter.

83. REPETITION AND TRUNCATION *Repeat notes or leave them out.*

Original Melody to "When The Saints Go Marching In." (this excerpt is not on the recording)
ALTO SAX
BARITONE SAX
TENOR SAX
TRUMPET
TROMBONE
GUITAR
PIANO
BASS
DRUMS
C TREBLE/
VIBES
A. SAX
B. SAX
T. SAX
TPT.
TBN.
GTR.
PNO.
BASS
DMS.
C/VIB.

84. SAINTS REINVENTED *Compare this reinvented version with the original melody.*

Repetition
Truncation
1.
2.
A. SAX
B. SAX
T. SAX
TPT.
TBN.
GTR.
PNO.
BASS
DMS.
C/VIB.

Student Book Page 17

LESSON #2 Ornamenting Melody

Improvisation Concept – *Improvising by adding notes to a melody (Ornamentation).*

All Lesson #2 exercises are played with Straight 8ths.

85. SIMPLE SHOO FLY *Start with a simple familiar melody.*

86. NEIGHBOR TONES *Add notes below or above the melody.*

87. PASSING TONES *Add notes between the melody notes.*

88. ENCLOSING TONES *Add notes above and below the melody. Usually a step or half step above and a half step below.*

89. CHROMATIC APPROACH TONES *Add notes a half step away from the melody.*

90. DOUBLE CHROMATIC APPROACH TONES *Add two chromatic notes to a melody.*

ALTO SAX
BARITONE SAX
TENOR SAX
TRUMPET
TROMBONE
GUITAR
PIANO
BASS
DRUMS
C TREBLE/
VIBES

A. SAX
B. SAX
T. SAX
TPT.
TBN.
GTR.
PNO.
BASS
DMS.
C/VIB.

Student Book Page 17

91. ORNAMENTING SAINTS

"When The Saints Go Marching In" with ornaments.

Enclosure(s)
Passing Tones
1.
2.
A. SAX
B. SAX
T. SAX
TPT.
TBN.
GTR.
PNO.
BASS
DMS.
C/VIB.

PERFORMANCE SPOTLIGHT *The Saints Are Swingin' Low*

New Orleans, generally recognized as the birthplace of jazz, was a major economic and cultural center in the southern United States at the beginning of the 20th century. The very first jazz ensembles were the brass bands that played in a ragtime style. Famous musicians from New Orleans include:

Buddy Bolden	Sidney Bechet	Fats Domino	Dr. John
Louis Armstrong	Wynton Marsalis	Professor Longhair	The Dirty Dozen Brass Band
Jelly Roll Morton	Harry Connick Jr.	Louis Prima	Terence Blanchard

Additional Teacher Information

The Saints Are Swinging Low – New Orleans

In New Orleans, at the end of the 1800s and the beginning of the 20th century, the descendants of slaves and "Creoles of Color" fashioned a new kind of music. It was a blend of various musical styles and genres such as the Blues, African American church music, marching band music, ragtime, and slave hollers (field songs) which later became known as jazz. Early New Orleans jazz style features group improvisation and a "loose" or relaxed rhythmic feel known as "second line":

Suggested Video Resources:
Ken Burns Jazz – Episode One "Gumbo"

Suggested Listening:
Potato Head Blues by Louis Armstrong
Heebie Jeebies by Louis Armstrong
Livery Stable Blues by the Original Dixieland Jazz Band
Dead Man Blues by Jelly Roll Morton

Rhythmic Concept – *"**Second Line Rhythmic Feel**" is a style of drumming that originated in New Orleans. The 8th notes in a "**Second Line**" feel are played between what would be straight 8ths and regular triplet-oriented swing 8th notes.*

92. STRAIGHT, SWING AND SECOND LINE 8TH NOTES

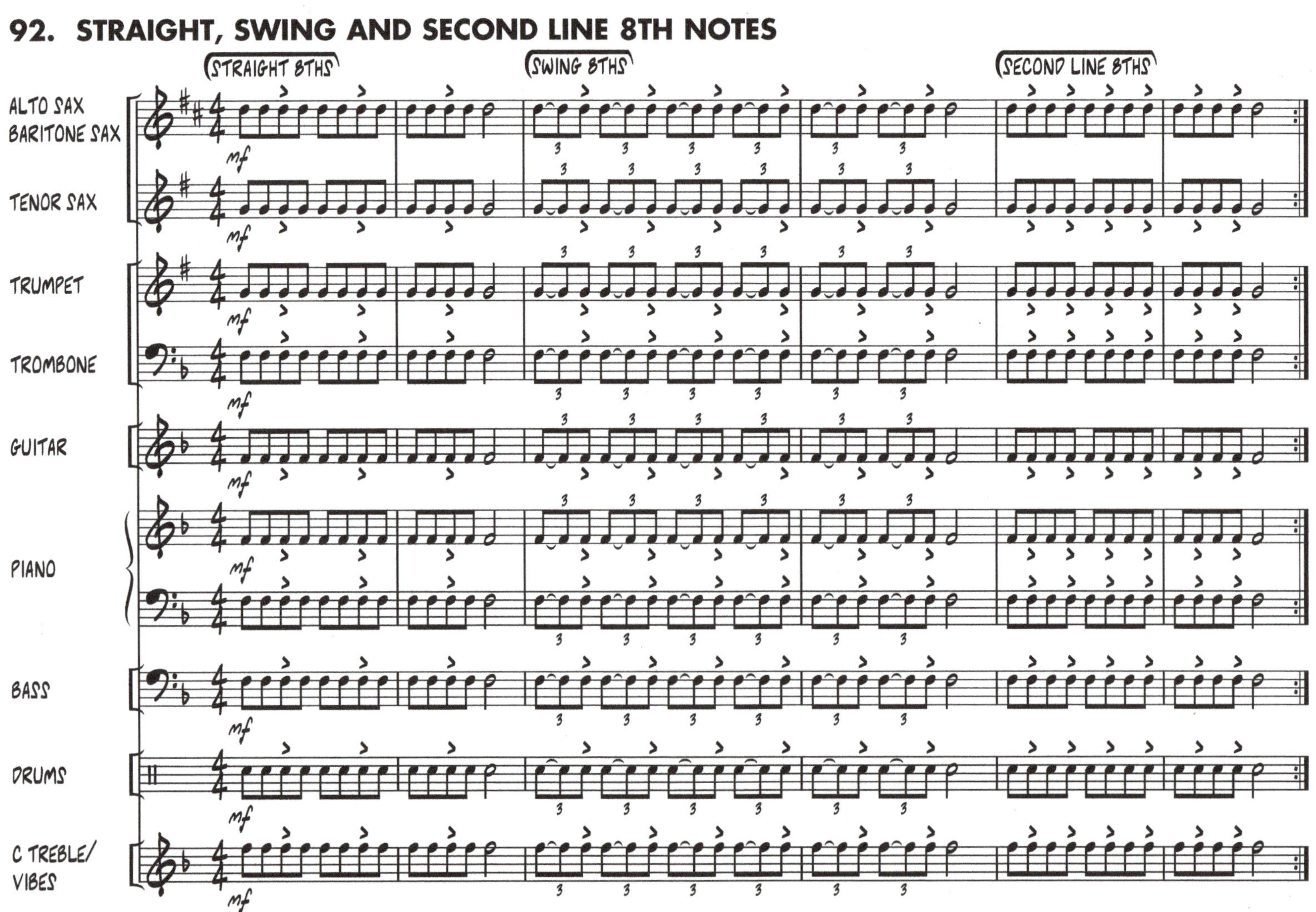

Rhythmic Concept – ***Tresillo Rhythm*** *is a three note rhythm which is very common in New Orleans music and early Rock 'n' Roll.*

93. WORKOUT FOR RHYTHMIC FEEL AND GROOVE

94. MELODY WORKOUT FOR "SAINTS"

95. MELODY WORKOUT FOR "SWING LOW"

96. THE SAINTS ARE SWINGIN' LOW – Full Band Arrangement

17
A. SAX
T. SAX
B. SAX
TPT.
TBN.
GTR.
PNO.
BASS
DMS.
C/VIB.
1. 2.
PLAY 2ND TIME ONLY
3.
mf

26
(SOLOS)*
D6
A9
G6
D9
C9
F6
C7
A. SAX
T. SAX
B. SAX
TPT.
TBN.
GTR.
PNO.
BASS
DMS.
C/VIB.
R R L R R L R L
34
G9
Bb9
(SIM.)
*CLEAR NOTEHEADS = CHORD TONES

A. SAX
T. SAX
B. SAX
TPT.
TBN.
GTR.
PNO.
BASS
DMS.
C/VIB.
REPEAT FOR MORE SOLOS
TO CONTINUE
43
51
D6
G6
F6
F13
E13 F13
C9
B9 C9
DIV.
SIM.

Student Book Page 19

This page left intentionally blank

97. DEMONSTRATION SOLO FOR "THE SAINTS ARE SWINGIN' LOW"

98. PRACTICE TRACK FOR "THE SAINTS ARE SWINGIN' LOW" – mm. 26-42 (3 choruses)

Student Book Page 20

LESSON #3 Blues Riffs

Improvisation Concept – ***Riffs*** *are short melodies that are common parts of jazz solos often using notes of the blues scales (minor and major). Blues songs and solos often use three identical four-bar riffs.*

All Lesson #3 exercises are played in a Swing style.

99. BLUES RIFF #1 *Blues Riff played 3 times over a twelve-bar blues.*

100. BLUES RIFF #2

Theory Concept – *Often the 3rd of the key is flatted to fit better with the IV chord.*

101. "ROVING THIRD" RIFF #1

102. "ROVING THIRD" RIFF #2

▼ *This note is flatted to fit the chord.*

103. "ROVING THIRD" RIFF #3

104. "ROVING THIRD" RIFF #4

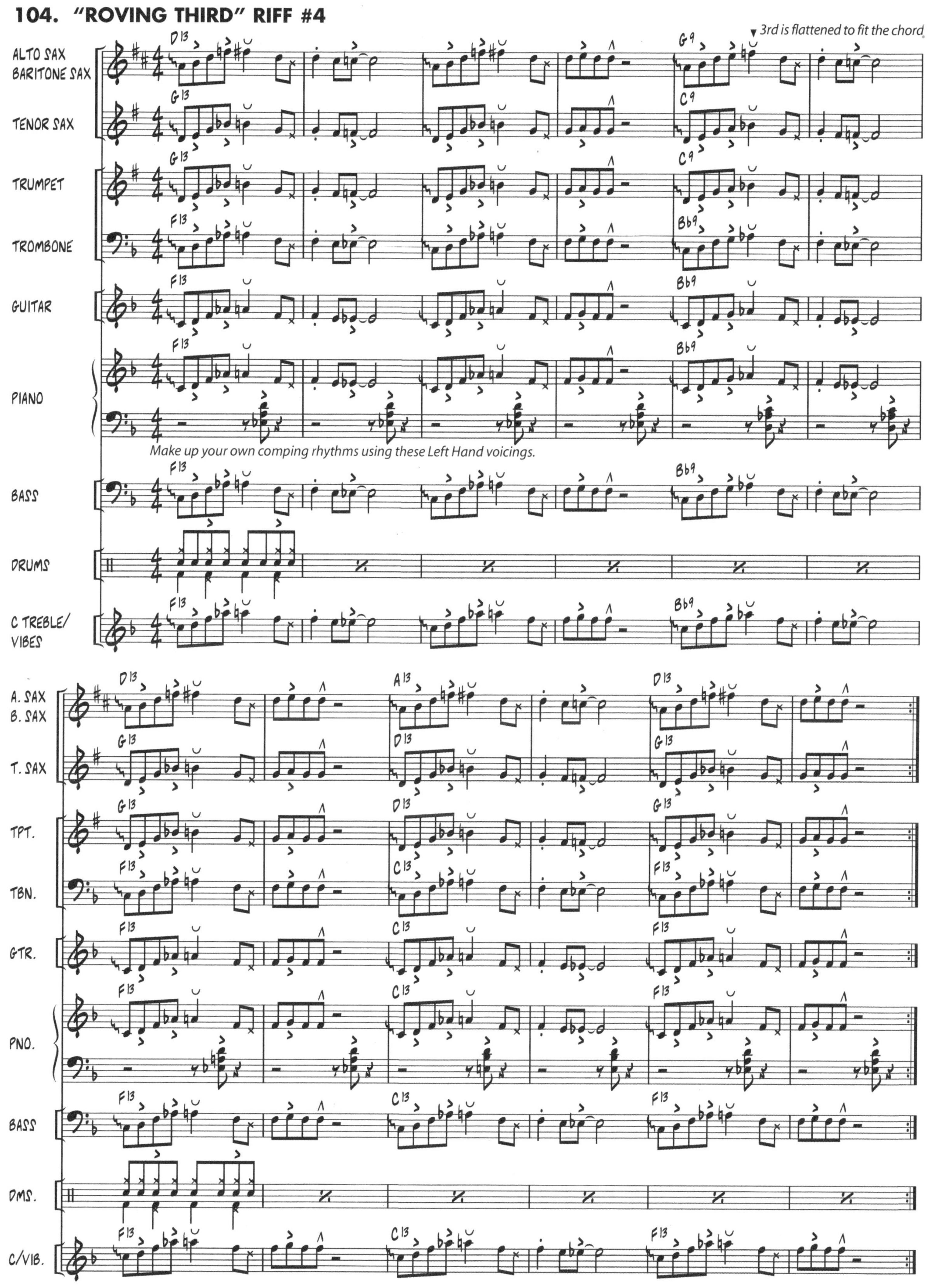

Student Book Page 21

LESSON #4 *Call and Response*

Improvisation Concept – ***Call and Response*** *is a traditional way of playing or singing melodies common in African American Church music of the 19th and 20th centuries.*

All Lesson #4 exercises are played in a Swing style.

105. CALL AND RESPONSE #1

106. CALL AND RESPONSE #2

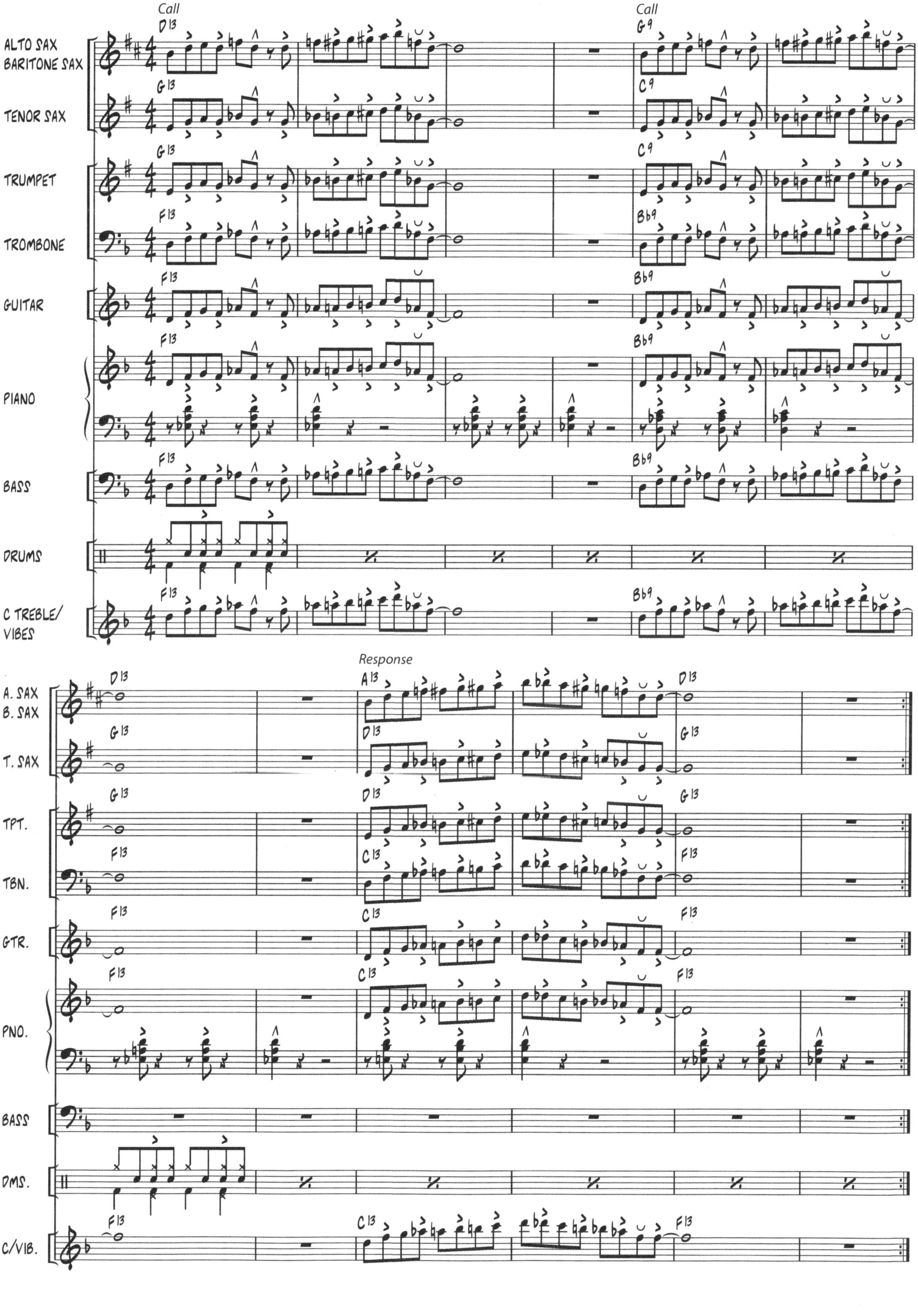

Call

Call

ALTO SAX
BARITONE SAX

TENOR SAX

TRUMPET

TROMBONE

GUITAR

PIANO

BASS

DRUMS

C TREBLE/
VIBES

Response

A. SAX
B. SAX

T. SAX

TPT.

TBN.

GTR.

PNO.

BASS

DMS.

C/VIB.

107. CALL AND RESPONSE #3

Student Book Page 21

Improvisation Concept – *Improvising using Short Call and Response Riffs. Often songs and solos use two-bar phrases in a "Call and Response" style. The responses usually start in bars 3, 7, and 11 and are similar or identical.*

108. CALL AND RESPONSE #4

Play 3 Times – Listen, play, then improvise by changing the rhythm.

109. CALL AND RESPONSE #5

Play 3 Times – Listen, play, then improvise by changing the rhythm.

PERFORMANCE SPOTLIGHT *Vine Street Ruckus*

In the 1930s **Kansas City** was home to some of the greatest musicians in jazz. Bands led by Count Basie and Jay McShann played a swing style of music that drew heavily on the blues tradition of "Call and Response." Important musicians from or associated with Kansas City Jazz:

Charlie Parker	Claude Williams	Buck Clayton	Hot Lips Page	Count Basie
Bobby Watson	Coleman Hawkins	Lester Young	Jay McShann	Pat Metheny
Bob Brookmeyer	Ben Webster	Andy Kirk	Mary Lou Williams	Jimmy Rushing
Walter Page	Jimmy Lunceford	Hershel Evans	Big Joe Turner	Bennie Moten

Additional Teacher Information

Vine Street Ruckus – Kansas City

Jazz music spread quickly as musicians travelled from New Orleans to other cities. Excursion riverboats provided musical entertainment as they stopped at various cities on the Mississippi, Missouri, and Ohio Rivers. Kansas City became a hotbed for a style of jazz music that drew heavily from the blues. Early important bands such as Walter Page's Blue Devils, Andy Kirk's Clouds of Joy, and the Bennie Moten Orchestra travelled throughout Missouri, Kansas, Oklahoma and Texas spreading the music to towns and cities not accessible by waterways. Kansas City bands were often bigger than early jazz bands and the "Kansas City Style" exploited short bluesy melodies called riffs that were often made up spontaneously by members of various sections in the band.

Suggested Video Resources:
Ken Burns Jazz – Episode Five "The Velocity of Swing"

Suggested Listening:
Moten Swing by Bennie Moten & The Kansas City Orchestra
Jumpin' At The Woodside by Count Basie
Lester Leaps In by the Kansas City Seven
Oh, Lady Be Good by Jones-Smith, Inc.

110. MELODY WORKOUT #1 – Main Riff

111. MELODY WORKOUT #2 – Response Riff

112. "VINE STREET RUCKUS" – Full Band Arrangement

A. SAX
T. SAX
B. SAX
TPT.
TBN.
GTR.
PNO.
BASS
DMS.
C/VIB.
DIV.
F6
Db9
C9SUS
C7SUS
19
mf
PLAY 2ND TIME ONLY
Bb7
Bb13

A. SAX
T. SAX
B. SAX
TPT.
TBN.
GTR.
PNO.
BASS
DMS.
C/VIB.
F6
Db9
C9SUS
DIV.
1.
2.
33
F9SUS
Bb13
ff

A. SAX
T. SAX
B. SAX
TPT.
TBN.
GTR.
PNO.
BASS
DMS.
C/VIB.
DIV.
mf
ff
F6
Bb SUS
Bb13
FINE
SOLO BREAK
Db9(#11)
C7(#9)
F#13
F13

45
OPEN FOR SOLOS *
OPT. RIFF FROM M. 7 AS BACKGROUND (ON CUE)
A. SAX
T. SAX
B. SAX
TPT.
TBN.
GTR.
PNO.
BASS
DMS.
C/VIB.
D9
G9
C9
F9
Bb9
A9
COMP IF NOT SOLOING
F13
mf
Make up your own comping rhythms using these voicings.
WALK
SIM.
*CLEAR NOTEHEADS = CHORD TONES

57
A. SAX
T. SAX
B. SAX
TPT.
TBN.
GTR.
PNO.
BASS
DMS.
C/VIB.
DIV.
COMP
F6
Bb7
F9
Bb9
D.S. AL FINE
Db9
C9SUS
F9SUS
C9
f
ff
mf

113. DEMONSTRATION SOLO FOR "VINE STREET RUCKUS"

114. PRACTICE TRACK FOR "VINE STREET RUCKUS" – mm. 45-56 (4 choruses)

Student Book Page 24

LESSON #5 Mixolydian Vamp and Chromatic Passing Tones

Theory Concept – *Many jazz songs are written using the Mixolydian Mode. Interesting vamps can be made by building a chord on each note of the mode. A* ***"Vamp"*** *is a repeated musical pattern.*

All Lesson #5 exercises are played with Straight 8ths.

115. MIXOLYDIAN WORKOUT #1

Listen the first time then play any note in the chords on the repeat.

116. MIXOLYDIAN WORKOUT #2

117. IMPROVISING ON MODAL VAMPS *Jazz solos can be improvised over modal vamps by using the notes of the basic mode.*

Improvisation Concept – *Chromatic Passing Tones can be added to a mode between the whole steps.*

Whole Step *Whole Step* *Half Step* *Whole Step* *Whole Step* *Half Step* *Whole Step*

ALTO SAX
BARITONE SAX
TENOR SAX
TRUMPET
TROMBONE
GUITAR
PIANO
BASS
DRUMS
C TREBLE/
VIBES

118. ADDING CHROMATIC NOTES

Keep the notes of the mode on downbeats (when adding passing tones) to create a smooth and jazzy sound.

ALTO SAX
BARITONE SAX
TENOR SAX
TRUMPET
TROMBONE
GUITAR
PIANO
BASS
DRUMS
C TREBLE/
VIBES

119. PASSING TONE WORKOUT #1

120. PASSING TONE WORKOUT #2

121. PASSING TONE WORKOUT #3

LESSON #6 Composite Blues Scale

Theory Concept – ***The Composite Blues Scale*** *is formed by combining the Minor Blues Scale and the Major Blues Scale. The Composite Blues Scale has 9 different notes.*

Student Book Page 25

All Lesson #6 exercises are played with Straight 8ths.

122. THEORY WORKOUT *Compare the Minor, Major, and Composite Blues Scales.*

123. COMPOSITE BLUES SCALE WORKOUT #1

124. COMPOSITE BLUES SCALE WORKOUT #2

125. COMPOSITE BLUES SCALE WORKOUT #3

Student Book Page 26

PERFORMANCE SPOTLIGHT *Beale Street Barbeque*

On December 15, 1977, **Beale Street** (in Memphis, TN) was officially declared the "Home of the Blues" by an act of the U.S. Congress. Memphis was an important music center throughout the 20th century and Memphis musicians influenced all types of American music including jazz, blues, soul, gospel and Rock 'n' Roll. Famous musicians associated with Memphis include:

Elvis Presley	Howlin' Wolf	Booker T. Jones	Memphis Minnie	W.C. Handy
Aretha Franklin	B.B. King	Isaac Hayes	Booker Little	George Coleman

Additional Teacher Information

Beale Street Barbeque – Memphis

Memphis is located on the Mississippi River 400 miles north of New Orleans. Two of the most important jazz musicians associated with Memphis are Jimmy Lunceford and W. C. Handy. While neither was born in Memphis, both settled there for a time and organized bands that performed on Beale Street, which became (and remains) a popular center for many types of music. W. C. Handy is extremely important in the history of jazz because he was the first to notate (write down) the blues.

Suggested Video Resources:

Ken Burns Jazz – Episode Five "The Velocity of Swing"

Suggested Listening:

Memphis Blues by Jim Europe's Infantry Band
composed by W. C. Handy

For Dancers Only by Jimmy Lunceford

St. Louis Blues by Louis Armstrong
composed by W. C. Handy

Lunceford Special by Jimmy Lunceford

126. MELODY WORKOUT

A. SAX
B. SAX
T. SAX
TPT.
TBN.
GTR.
PNO.
BASS
DMS.
C/VIB.
2
2
A. SAX
B. SAX
T. SAX
TPT.
TBN.
GTR.
PNO.
BASS
DMS.
C/VIB.
2
2

A. SAX
B. SAX
T. SAX
TPT.
TBN.
GTR.
PNO.
BASS
DMS.
C/VIB.

127. RHYTHM WORKOUT – Bass Vamp

(STRAIGHT 8THS)

ALTO SAX
BARITONE SAX
TENOR SAX
TRUMPET
TROMBONE
GUITAR
PIANO
BASS
DRUMS
C TREBLE/ VIBES

128. "BEALE STREET BARBEQUE" – Full Band Arrangement

17
DIV.
A. SAX
T. SAX
B. SAX
TPT.
TBN.
(Bb13)
GTR.
PNO.
BASS
DMS.
C/VIB.
Db/Eb
Db/E

25

A. SAX
T. SAX
B. SAX
TPT.
TBN.
(Db/Eb) D/E Eb/F Db/Eb D/E Eb/F Db/Eb D/E Eb/F
GTR.
(Db/Eb) D/E Eb/F Db/Eb D/E Eb/F Db6/Eb D6/E Eb6/F
PNO.
BASS
DMS.
C/VIB.

TO CODA ⊕

PLAY 1ST TIME ONLY

A. SAX
T. SAX
B. SAX
PLAY 1ST TIME ONLY
TPT.
TBN.
Bb13
GTR.
PNO.
BASS
DMS.
PLAY 1ST TIME ONLY
C/VIB.

Student Book Page 26 and 27

35 (OPEN FOR SOLOS) *

Suggested Scale Material: Composite Blues Scale

A. SAX G13

T. SAX C13

B. SAX G13

TPT. C13

TBN. Bb13

GTR. Bb13 (COMP IF NOT SOLOING)

PNO. (SIM.)

BASS (SIM.)

DMS.

C/VIB. Bb13

FOR MORE CHORUSES | TO CONTINUE

(SOLI) 44

f

(ENS.)

(SOLI)

*CLEAR NOTEHEADS = CHORD TONES

A. SAX
T. SAX
B. SAX
TPT.
TBN.
GTR.
PNO.
BASS
DMS.
C/VIB.
52

D.S. AL CODA
A. SAX
T. SAX
B. SAX
TPT.
TBN.
GTR.
PNO.
BASS
DMS.
FLOOR TOM
C/VIB.
CODA
DIV.
GMI FMI GMI FMI GMI FMI GMI FMI Eb FMI

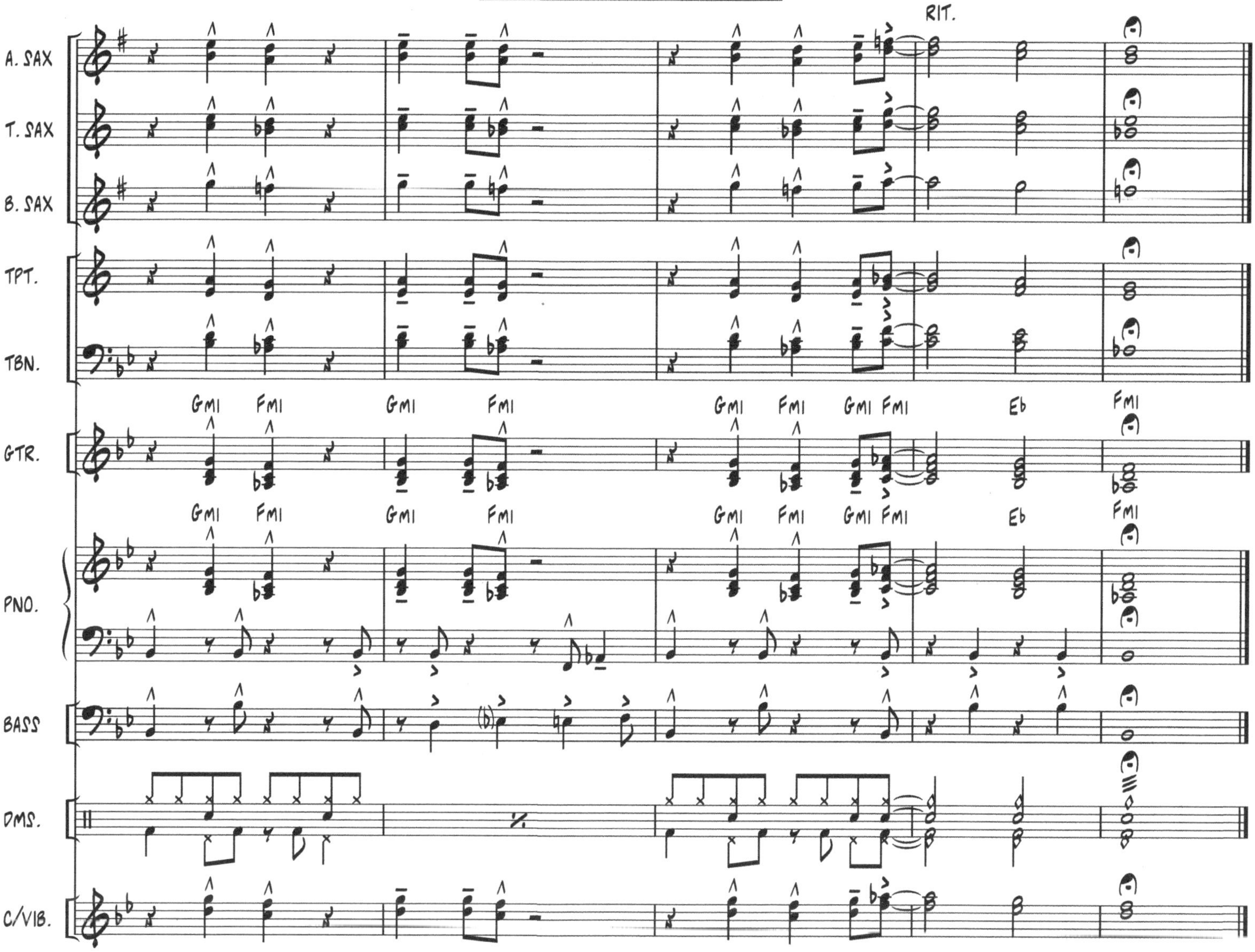
RIT.
A. SAX
T. SAX
B. SAX
TPT.
TBN.
GTR.
GMI FMI GMI FMI GMI FMI GMI FMI Eb FMI
PNO.
GMI FMI GMI FMI GMI FMI GMI FMI Eb FMI
BASS
DMS.
C/VIB.

129. DEMONSTRATION SOLO FOR "BEALE STREET BARBEQUE"

STRAIGHT 8THS
35-1
C TREBLE
Bb INSTR.
Eb INSTR.
BASS CLEF
DRUMS

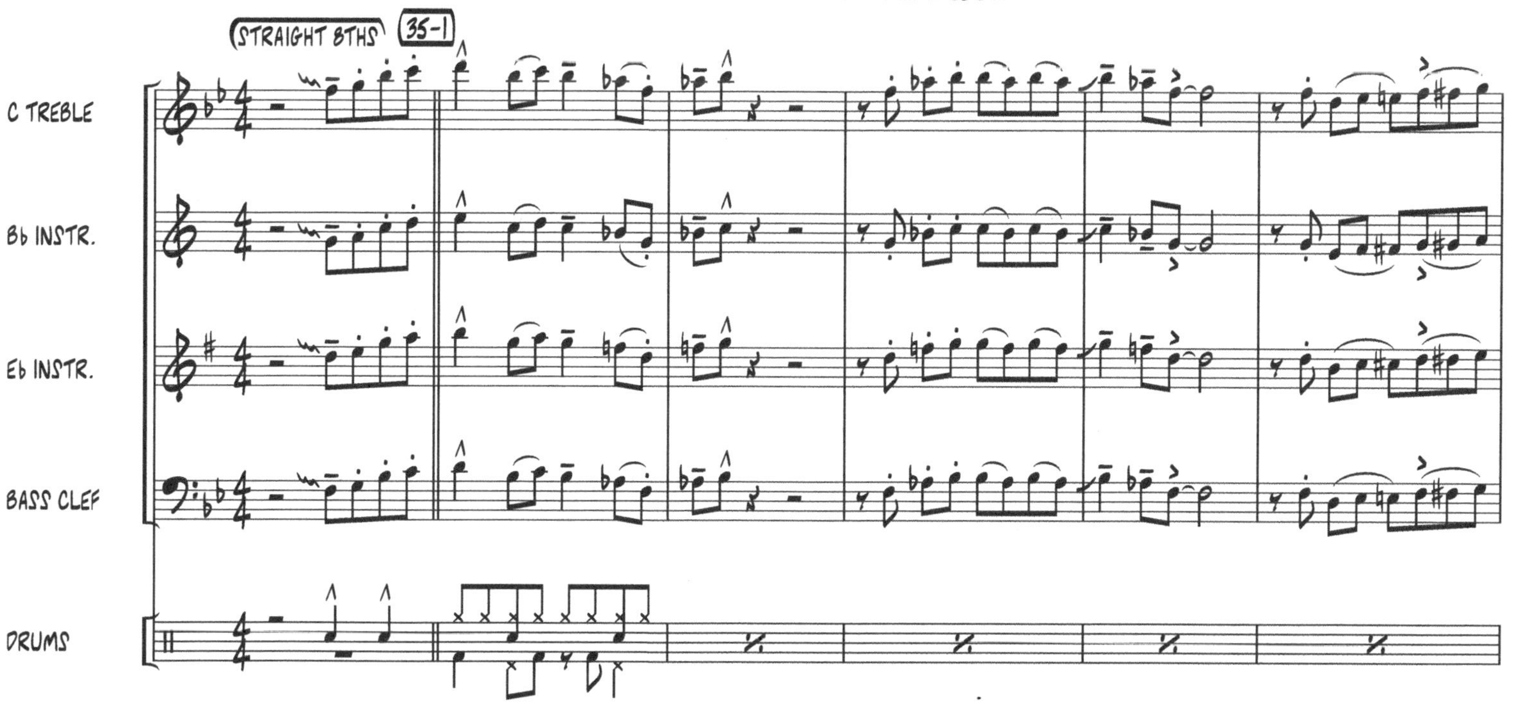

130. PRACTICE TRACK FOR "BEALE STREET BARBEQUE" – mm. 35-42 (6 choruses)

LESSON #7 Triplets in Swing and Dorian Vamp

Improvisation Concept – *Triplets are very important in making jazz swing. Often the underlying rhythmic subdivision in swing is the triplet. Not all music in a swing feel is interpreted as a strict triplet. Generally at faster tempos the 8ths are more equal in value.*

All Lesson #7 exercises are played in a Swing style.

131. TRIPLET WORKOUT #1

132. TRIPLET WORKOUT #2

133. TRIPLET WORKOUT #3

Student Book Page 28

Theory Review – The Major Scale has seven modes. *Each mode is built on a different note of the scale. Each mode has a unique sound, unique name, and works well with a specific chord type. Ionian is another name for the Major Scale.*

134. SEVEN MODES OF THE MAJOR SCALE (Concert B♭)

Play each of the modes while listening to the related chords.

Theory Concept – Modal Vamp Using The Dorian Mode (2nd Mode). *Many jazz songs are written using the Dorian Mode. Interesting vamps can be made by building a chord on each note of the mode.*

135. DORIAN WORKOUT

Play the mode then pick any note in the chords.

Student Book Page 29

LESSON #8 Dorian Vamp and Minor Pentatonic Scale

136. DORIAN VAMP

Listen the first time then play any note in the chords on the repeat.

137. DORIAN WORKOUT WITH TRIPLETS

138. DORIAN MODE – 9th, 6th, and 11th

Theory Review – Pentatonic Scales have five notes. *There are two basic pentatonic scales: Major Pentatonic and Minor Pentatonic. The Minor Pentatonic sounds very similar to the Dorian Mode.*

139. DORIAN/MINOR PENTATONIC

140. MINOR PENTATONIC WORKOUT WITH TRIPLETS

PERFORMANCE SPOTLIGHT *Windy City*

Musicians from New Orleans such as Joe "King" Oliver and Louis Armstrong brought jazz to **Chicago** in the 1920s and became important influences for the local musicians. The "Windy City" quickly became an important center for jazz music and remains so today. Some important musicians from Chicago include:

Paul Butterfield	Nat King Cole	Jack DeJohnette	Kurt Elling	Chaka Khan	Benny Goodman
Lester Bowie	Bud Freeman	Dinah Washington	Herbie Hancock	Gene Krupa	Ramsey Lewis
Chicago (The Band)	Lou Rawls	Lennie Tristano	Jimmy McPartland	Lil Hardin Armstrong	Buddy Guy

Additional Teacher Information

Windy City – Chicago

King Oliver brought his jazz band to Chicago in 1918 just one year after the first jazz recordings had been made. In 1922 he added Louis Armstrong to the band. Their New Orleans style of collective improvisation became popular with black and white audiences. Quickly, young white musicians in Chicago, namely clarinetist Benny Goodman, Frankie Trumbauer, Jimmy McPartland, and Bix Biederbeck began imitating the music and the musicians they admired. Since the 1920s Chicago has remained an important center for jazz.

Suggested Video Resources:
Ken Burns Jazz - Episode 2 "The Gift"
- Episode 3 "Our Language"

Suggested Listening:
Chimes Blues by King Oliver
Riverboat Shuffle by Frankie Trumbauer
Singin' the Blues by Frankie Trumbauer
King Porter Stomp by Benny Goodman
Rose Room by Benny Goodman
Tanya Jean by Kurt Elling

141. RHYTHM WORKOUT

A. SAX
B. SAX
Doo Doo Bah
Doo Dot Doo Bah
Doo Doo Bah
Doo Dot Doo Bah
T. SAX
TPT.
TBN.
GTR.
PNO.
BASS
DMS.
C/VIB.
A. SAX
B. SAX
Doo Doo Bah Dot Doo Bah
Dot Doo Bah Doo Bah Doo Bah
it. Doo Bah
it.
T. SAX
TPT.
TBN.
GTR.
PNO.
BASS
DMS.
C/VIB.

142. MELODY WORKOUT

Student Book Page 30

144. "WINDY CITY" – Full Band Arrangement

A. SAX
T. SAX
B. SAX
TPT.
TBN.
GTR.
PNO.
BASS
MAKE UP YOUR OWN COMPING RHYTHM WHILE MAINTAINING THE BASIC GROOVE.
DMS.
(SIM.)
C/VIB.
17

Student Book Page 31

CODA
PLAY 3 TIMES
DIV.
1. 2.
3.
A. SAX
T. SAX
B. SAX
TPT.
TBN.
GTR.
PNO.
BASS
DMS.
PLAY LAST TIME ONLY
C/VIB.

145. DEMONSTRATION SOLO FOR "WINDY CITY"

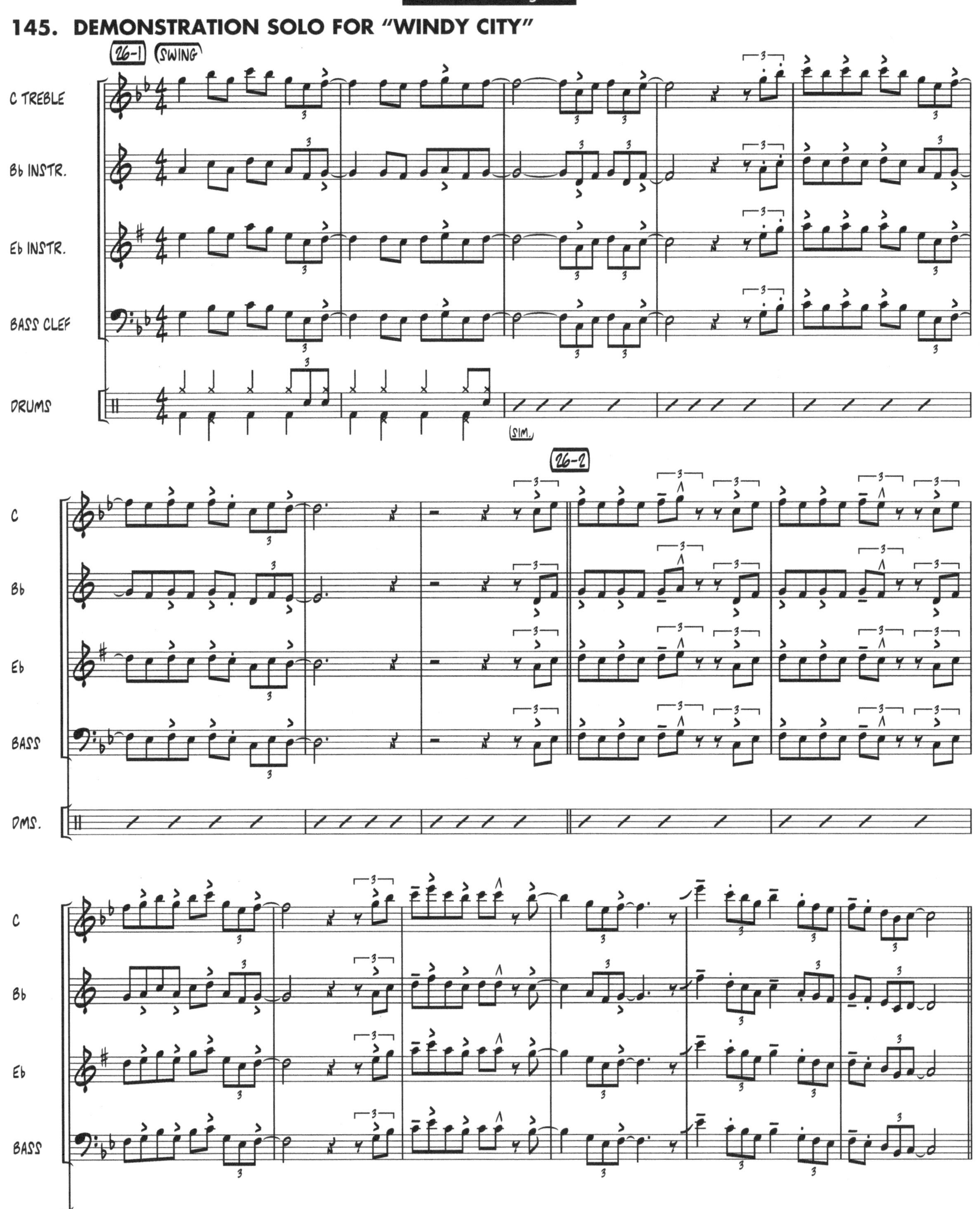

146. PRACTICE TRACK FOR "WINDY CITY" – mm. 26-33 (4 choruses)

LESSON #9 Bebop Scale and Double-Time Playing

Theory Review – *Adding a note between the seventh and root of the Mixolydian mode produces a Bebop Scale. This was a common sound in the Bebop era and has been used in many jazz styles.*

All Lesson #9 exercises are played with Straight 8ths.

147. MIXOLYDIAN MODE/BEBOP SCALE

148. MIXOLYDIAN MODE/BEBOP SCALE WORKOUT

Theory Concept – *The* ***"Bebop Lick"*** *uses four 8th notes and three pitches. One of the notes is repeated.*

149. BEBOP LICK WORKOUT #1

150. BEBOP LICK WORKOUT #2

ALTO SAX
BARITONE SAX

TENOR SAX

TRUMPET

TROMBONE

GUITAR

PIANO

BASS

DRUMS

C TREBLE/
VIBES

Improvisation Concept – *At times the Bebop lick is played on a dissonant note to add tension to the music.*

151. BEBOP LICK WORKOUT #3

ALTO SAX
BARITONE SAX

TENOR SAX

TRUMPET

TROMBONE

GUITAR

PIANO

BASS

DRUMS

C TREBLE/
VIBES

Rhythmic Concept – ***Double Time*** *(or* ***"Doubling Up"****) is often played with 16th note rhythms. These will sound the same as 8th note rhythms at a faster tempo but with a "half time feel."*

152. DOUBLE-TIME WORKOUT #1

ALTO SAX
BARITONE SAX

TENOR SAX

TRUMPET

TROMBONE

GUITAR

PIANO

BASS

DRUMS

C TREBLE/
VIBES

153. DOUBLE-TIME WORKOUT #2

ALTO SAX
BARITONE SAX

TENOR SAX

TRUMPET

TROMBONE

GUITAR

PIANO

BASS

DRUMS

C TREBLE/
VIBES

154. DOUBLE-TIME WORKOUT #3

Student Book Page 33

LESSON #10 The Ten-Note Bebop Scale

Improvisation Concept – *Sometimes chromatic notes are added to the basic eight-note Bebop Scales.*

All Lesson #10 exercises are played with Straight 8ths.

155. TEN-NOTE MIXOLYDIAN BEBOP SCALE

156. TEN-NOTE MIXOLYDIAN BEBOP SCALE WORKOUT #1

157. TEN-NOTE MIXOLYDIAN BEBOP SCALE WORKOUT #2

158. ADDING CHROMATIC NOTES

Often the ♭3 is placed on a downbeat to create a bluesy effect.

Student Book Page 34

PERFORMANCE SPOTLIGHT *Baytown Boogaloo*

Tower Of Power has been one of the most successful jazz/rock fusion ensembles since the 1970s. Formed in Oakland, CA, their sound is a unique blend of Rhythm & Blues elements, precision horn section work, tightly constructed bass lines, and infectious drum grooves. Much of their music is played in a 16th note rock feel. "Baytown Boogaloo" is written in a *Tower of Power* style.

Additional Teacher Information

Baytown Boogaloo – Oakland, CA

Tower of Power was formed in 1970 and developed a unique style of music that is a blend of Rhythm and Blues, Funk, and Jazz Rock. The horn section of Tower of Power is renowned for its precision and has appeared on recordings of a number of other artists including Otis Redding, Aerosmith, Bonnie Raitt, David Sanborn, Elton John, Huey Lewis, and Heart.

Suggested Listening:
The Very Best of Tower of Power: The Warner Years by Tower of Power

159. 16TH NOTE WORKOUT

A. SAX
B. SAX
Doo Dot Doo Bah Dot Doo Dot Doo Bah Doo Bah Dit Dot Doo Dot Doo Dit Bah Dit Dot Doo Dot Bah Dit Dot
T. SAX
TPT.
TBN.
GTR.
PNO.
BASS
DMS.
C/VIB.
A. SAX
B. SAX
Doo Bah Dot Doo Bah Doo Bah Dit Dot Doo Dit Bah Dit Dot Bah Dit Dot
T. SAX
TPT.
TBN.
GTR.
PNO.
BASS
DMS.
C/VIB.

160. MELODY WORKOUT

A. SAX
B. SAX
Doo Bah Doo Bah Doo Dit Bah Dit Dot
Dot Dot Doo Dit Bah Dit Dot Bah
T. SAX
TPT.
TBN.
GTR.
PNO.
BASS
DMS.
C/VIB.
A. SAX
B. SAX
Doo Doo Bah Doo Dit Bah Doo Bah Doo Dit Bah
Bah Doo Bah Doo Dit
Bah Doo Bah Doo Dit Bah Dit Dot
T. SAX
TPT.
TBN.
GTR.
PNO.
BASS
DMS.
2
C/VIB.

161. "BAYTOWN BOOGALOO" – Full Band Arrangement

9
NO REPEAT ON D.C.
A. SAX
T. SAX
B. SAX
TPT.
TBN.
GTR.
PNO.
BASS
DMS.
C/VIB.
DIV.
PLAY 2ND TIME ONLY
F13
FILL

17

A. SAX
T. SAX
B. SAX
TPT.
TBN.
GTR.
PNO.
BASS
DMS.
C/VIB.

(PLAY BOTH TIMES)

(PLAY BOTH TIMES)

(PLAY BOTH TIMES)

FINE

(PLAY FIRST TIME ONLY)

(DIV.)

(PLAY FIRST TIME ONLY)

(PLAY FIRST TIME ONLY)

(ON FINE - ENS.)

(PLAY FIRST TIME ONLY)

A. SAX
T. SAX
B. SAX
TPT.
TBN.
GTR.
PNO.
BASS
DMS.
C/VIB.

25
OPEN FOR SOLOS
A. SAX
T. SAX
B. SAX
TPT.
TBN.
GTR.
PNO.
BASS
DMS.
C/VIB.
D13
G13
F13
COMP IF NOT SOLOING
SIM.
(D13)
(G13)
(F13)
D.C. AL FINE
FILL

162. DEMONSTRATION SOLO FOR "BAYTOWN BOOGALOO"

163. PRACTICE TRACK FOR "BAYTOWN BOOGALOO" – mm. 25-32 (4 choruses)

Student Book Page 36

LESSON #11 9th Chords and Chord Tone Soloing

Theory Concept – *The Dominant 7th* *Chord (see page 3) is the most common chord in jazz because it has a naturally "bluesy" sound. Often the 9th is added.*

All Lesson #11 exercises are played in a Swing style.

164. DOMINANT 7TH AND 9TH CHORDS

165. TYPICAL PROGRESSION USING DOMINANT 9TH CHORD

Student Book Page 36

Improvisation Concept – *Chord Tone Soloing*: *Jazz musicians use chord tones to make interesting solo melodies.*

166. CHORD TONE WORKOUT

Rhythmic Concept – *For rhythmic variety add Triplets and start on upbeats.*

167. TRIPLET ARPEGGIOS

Student Book Page 36

Improvisation Concept – *For melodic variety start on notes other than the root of the chord.*

168. ARPEGGIOS STARTING ON 3

169. ARPEGGIOS STARTING ON 9

Student Book Page 36

170. ARPEGGIOS STARTING ON 5

LESSON #12 Chromatic and Passing Tones

Improvisation Concept – *Adding chromatic ornamentation to simple arpeggios can make the chord tones more interesting and jazzy.*

All Lesson #12 exercises are played in a Swing style.

171. CHROMATIC TONE BELOW THE ROOT

Student Book Page 37

172. CHROMATIC TONE BELOW THE THIRD

173. STARTING ON THE UPBEAT AND ADDING A TRIPLET

174. CHROMATIC TONE BELOW THE FIFTH

175. CHROMATIC TONE BELOW THE NINTH

Improvisation Concept – *Using passing tones between chord tones is an effective melodic device. Avoid skipping between non-chord tones: 4 and 6.*

176. ADDING 2 BETWEEN 1 AND 3

177. ADDING 6 BETWEEN 5 AND 7

178. PASSING TONE WORKOUT

PERFORMANCE SPOTLIGHT *Liberty Bell Shuffle*

The Declaration of Independence was ratified in **Philadelphia** on July 4, 1776. Important jazz musicians from Philadelphia include:

John Coltrane	Philly Joe Jones	Michael Brecker	Randy Brecker	Clifford Brown	Stan Getz
Billie Holiday	Jimmy McGriff	Lee Morgan	McCoy Tyner	Stanley Clarke	Kenny Barron
Pat Martino	Bobby Timmons	Red Rodney	Jimmy Garrison	Sonny Fortune	Hank Mobley
Jimmy Smith	Archie Shepp	Rashied Ali			

Additional Teacher Information

Liberty Bell Shuffle – Philadelphia

During the First World War (1914–1918) more than 400,000 African Americans moved to northern cities in search of good jobs and better lives. By 1920 Philadelphia's African American population had grown to 220,000. Although New York and Chicago became the centers for jazz, Philadelphia and other towns in Pennsylvania became frequent stops for important jazz musicians. Soon young musicians in the "City of Brotherly Love" began to play jazz. The list of important jazz musicians from Philly is impressive and includes greats John Coltrane, Billie Holiday, Lee Morgan, Clifford Brown, and Stan Getz.

Suggested Video Resources:
John Coltrane Documentary: Chasing Trane

Suggested Listening:
Blue Trane by John Coltrane
In A Sentimental Mood by John Coltrane and Duke Ellington
Without Your Love by Billie Holiday
I Get A Kick Out Of You by Clifford Brown
Some Skunk Funk by the Brecker Brothers

179. MELODY WORKOUT

1.
2.
A. SAX
B. SAX
Dwee Bah Dot Doo Bow
Bah Doo Bah
Bah Doo Bah
Bah Doo Dot
Dot
Bah
T. SAX
TPT.
TBN.
GTR.
PNO.
BASS
DMS.
C/VIB.
A. SAX
B. SAX
Bah Doo Bah Doo Bah
Bah Doo Doowee Doo Bah
Bah Doo Doo Doo Dot
Bah
Bah Doo Doowee Doo Bah
T. SAX
TPT.
TBN.
GTR.
PNO.
BASS
DMS.
C/VIB.

A. SAX
B. SAX
Bah Doo Dot Bah Doo Bah Bah Doo Doo Dot Dot Dwee Bah Dot Doo Bow Dot
T. SAX
TPT.
TBN.
GTR.
PNO.
BASS
DMS.
C/VIB.
A. SAX
B. SAX
Doowee Bah Dot Doo Bow Dot Dwee Bah Dot Doo Bow Bah Doo Bah Bah Doo Bah Bah Doo Dot
T. SAX
TPT.
TBN.
GTR.
PNO.
BASS
ENS.
DMS.
Bah Doo Bah Bah Doo Bah Bah Doo Dot
C/VIB.

180. "LIBERTY BELL SHUFFLE" – Full Band Arrangement

A. SAX
T. SAX
B. SAX
TPT.
TBN.
GTR.
PNO.
BASS
DMS.
C/VIB.
PLAY BOTH TIMES
PLAY BOTH TIMES
mf
mf
mf
C9
F9
Bb13
1.
2.
18
DIV.
DIV.
Eb9
Bb13
C9

Student Book Page 38 and 39

34

(OPEN FOR SOLOS)*

A. SAX: G7, C7, A7, D7

T. SAX: C7, F7, D7, G7

B. SAX: G7, C7, A7, D7

TPT.: C7, F7, D7, G7

TBN.: Bb7, Eb7, C7, F7

GTR.: Bb13 (COMP IF NOT SOLOING), Eb9, C9, F9

PNO.: Bb13, Eb9, C9, F9

Make up your own comping rhythms using these suggested voicings.

BASS: (WALK) Bb13, Eb9, C13, F13

DMS.: (SIM.)

C/VIB.: Bb7, Eb7, C7, F7

A. SAX: G7

T. SAX: C7

B. SAX: G7

TPT.: C7

TBN.: Bb7

GTR.: Bb13, Eb9, Bb13

PNO.: Bb13, Eb9, Bb13

BASS: Bb13, (SIM.)

DMS.: (ENS.)

C/VIB.: Bb7

42 (DIV.) *f*

*CLEAR NOTEHEADS = CHORD TONES

50

A. SAX
T. SAX
B. SAX
TPT.
TBN.
GTR. Eb9 C13 F9SUS F13 Bb13
PNO. Eb9 C13 F9SUS F13 Bb13
BASS
DMS. (SIM.)
C/VIB.

mf

A. SAX
T. SAX
B. SAX
TPT.
TBN.
GTR. Eb9 C9 F9 Bb13
PNO. Eb9 C9 F9 Bb13
BASS
DMS.
C/VIB.

D.C. AL FINE

181. DEMONSTRATION SOLO FOR "LIBERTY BELL SHUFFLE"

34-1 SWING

C TREBLE

Bb INSTR.

Eb INSTR.

BASS CLEF

DRUMS

SIM.

34-2

C

Bb

Eb

BASS

DMS.

C

Bb

Eb

BASS

DMS.

182. PRACTICE TRACK FOR "LIBERTY BELL SHUFFLE" – mm. 34-41 (4 choruses)

LESSON #13 ii–V–I in Major and Minor

Theory Concept – *Chord Function in Major and Minor*. *A chord can be built on each step of the major and minor scales. The chords are often labeled using Roman Numerals.*

All Lesson #13 exercises are played with Straight 8ths.

183. CHORDS OF MAJOR AND RELATIVE MINOR KEYS

Relative Minor has the same notes and key signature as Major but starts on the 6th note of the Major scale.

Theory Concept – *Two common chord progressions are ii-V-I in Major and ii-V-I in Minor. In B♭ Major the ii chord is CMI7, the V chord is F7, and I is B♭MA7. In G Minor the ii chord is AMI7♭5, the V chord is D7♭9, and I is GMI7. (Often the Major version includes the IV chord: ii-V-I-IV).*

184. ARPEGGIOS OF ii–V–I–IV IN MAJOR AND ii–V–I IN THE RELATIVE MINOR

Listen to the chords and play the arpeggios.

185. IMPROVISATION WORKOUT – Scales over ii–V–I–IV in Major

Student Book Page 40

Improvisation Concept – *Scale Bracketing* – *If the progression stays in one key the scale of that key can often be used as melodic material. Listen to the scale over the entire progression. Some notes may sound a bit dissonant.*

186. MAJOR SCALE OVER THE ENTIRE ii–V–I–IV IN MAJOR

LESSON #14 *Scale Bracketing*

Theory Concept – Scale Bracketing with the Dorian Scale: *The C Dorian mode works with* CMI7 *(ii) and also* F7 *(V). Likewise the B♭ Major scale works with* B♭MA7 *(I) and also* E♭MA7 *(IV).*

All Lesson #14 exercises are played with Straight 8ths.

187. DORIAN MODE AND MAJOR SCALE OVER ii–V–I–IV

Improvisation Concept – *Scale Bracketing in Minor:* *The Minor scale works well over ii and I chord, but Harmonic Minor sounds better with V chord (it has ♭9 of the V chord).*

188. MINOR SCALE AND HARMONIC MINOR SCALE OVER ii–V–I

Theory Concept – *Raising the 7th note of the Minor Scale produces the Harmonic Minor scale.*

189. IMPROVISATION WORKOUT *Three scales for ii–V–I in Minor*

190. COMPARE THE MINOR SCALE AND THE HARMONIC MINOR SCALE

191. HARMONIC MINOR (starting on the 5th) AND MINOR SCALE OVER ii–V–I IN MINOR

PERFORMANCE SPOTLIGHT *Ipanema Dreamin'*

Ipanema is a famous beach in Rio de Janeiro, Brazil. The **Bossa Nova** is a type of Latin music which originated in Brazil and became very popular worldwide in the 1950s and 1960s. Antonio Carlos Jobim's "Girl From Ipanema" was a big pop hit for Stan Getz (tenor sax). In 1965 it won a *Grammy* for "Record of the Year". It is one of the three most often recorded songs in history. Notable musicians associated with the Bossa Nova:

Antonio Carlos Jobim	Astrud Gilberto	Joao Gilberto	Sergio Mendez
Edu Lobo	Luiz Bonfá	Roberto Menescal	Hermeto Pascoal

Additional Teacher Information

Ipanema Dreamin' – Brazil

Afro-Cuban jazz, one of many styles of Latin jazz, was introduced to American audiences in the 1940s notably with the collaborations of bebop trumpeter Dizzy Gillespie and Chano Pozo. Bossa Nova is a style of Brazilian dance music that became very popular in the U.S. in the 1960s. While it borrows elements from the Brazilian samba, such as a repeated ostinato rhythm called *clave,* it is generally more sedate and slower. American saxophonist Stan Getz, in his well- known collaborations with Antonio Carlos Jobim, Astrud Gilberto, and Joao Gilberto, was instrumental in popularizing this mesmerizing style in the States.

Suggested Listening:

Jazz Samba (album) by Stan Getz
Getz/Gilberto (album) by Stan Getz
Getz Au Go Go (album) by Stan Getz
Luiz Bonfá Plays and Sings Bossa Nova by Luiz Bonfá

192. MELODY WORKOUT

A. SAX
B. SAX
T. SAX
TPT.
TBN.
GTR.
PNO.
BASS
DMS.
C/VIB.
PLAY 1ST TIME ONLY
A. SAX
B. SAX
T. SAX
TPT.
TBN.
GTR.
PNO.
BASS
DMS.
PLAY 1ST TIME ONLY
C/VIB.

Student Book Page 42 and 43

193. "IPANEMA DREAMIN'" – Full Band Arrangement

13
A. SAX
T. SAX
B. SAX
TPT.
TBN.
GTR.
PNO.
BASS
DMS.
C/VIB.
DIV.
AMI7(b5)
D7(b9)
GMI9
SIM.
21
NO REPEAT ON D.C.
CMI11
COMP
F7
BbMA7
EbMA7
mp

29

A. SAX
T. SAX
B. SAX
TPT.
TBN.
GTR.
PNO.
BASS
DMS.
C/VIB.

(EbMA7) Ami7(b5) D7(b9) Gmi9

37

PLAY 1ST TIME ONLY

TO CODA

A. SAX
T. SAX
B. SAX
TPT.
TBN.
GTR.
PNO.
BASS
DMS.
C/VIB.

(Gmi9) Cmi11 F7 BbMA7 EbMA7 Ami7(b5) D7(b9) Gmi7

f

41
OPEN FOR SOLOS *
A. SAX
T. SAX
B. SAX
TPT.
TBN.
GTR.
PNO.
BASS
DMS.
C/VIB.
AMI7
D7
GMA7
DMI7
G7
CMA7
CMI7
F7
BbMA7
CMI11
COMP IF NOT SOLOING
Make up your own comping rhythms using these suggested voicings.
SIM.
49
FMA7
F#MI7(b5)
B7(b9)
EMI6/9
BMI7(b5)
E7(b9)
AMI6/9
EbMA7
AMI7(b5)
D7(b9)
GMI6/9
*CLEAR NOTEHEADS = CHORD TONES

D.C. AL CODA
CODA
RIT.
A. SAX
T. SAX
B. SAX
TPT.
TBN.
GTR.
PNO.
BASS
DMS.
C/VIB.
AMI7(b5) D7(b9) GMI7
TIME WITH LIGHT FILLS

194. DEMONSTRATION SOLO FOR "IPANEMA DREAMIN'"

49-2

C: BbMA7 · EbMA7 · AMI7(b5) · D7(b9) · GMI6/9

Bb: CMA7 · FMA7 · BMI7(b5) · E7(b9) · AMI6/9

Eb: GMA7 · CMA7 · F#MI7(b5) · B7(b9) · EMI6/9

BASS: BbMA7 · EbMA7 · AMI7(b5) · D7(b9) · GMI6/9

DMS.

195. PRACTICE TRACK FOR "IPANEMA DREAMIN'" – mm. 41-56 (4 choruses)

PERFORMANCE SPOTLIGHT *Skating In The Park*

The **Modern Jazz Quartet** was one of the most successful small ensembles in the "modern jazz era." **Skating In Central Park** by pianist John Lewis is one of their most famous compositions. "Skating In The Park" is a tribute to that song and to New York City, the home of Central Park. New York City became the most important center for jazz music in the last half of the 20th century. Nearly all the great jazz musicians in history have performed at New York's most famous jazz clubs: The Village Vanguard, The Blue Note, the Savoy Ballroom, the Village Gate, the Five Spot, and Birdland.

Additional Teacher Information

Skating in the Park – New York City

This song is both a tribute to New York City, which remains the most important center for jazz music, and to The Modern Jazz Quintet and its leader John Lewis. The MJQ played music that used elements from classical music, bebop, and cool jazz. New York City became a destination for jazz lovers as much for its famous venues as its musicians. Visitors and locals could be assured that they would hear the finest jazz in the world at Roseland, The Savoy Ballroom, The Cotton Club, The Village Gate, The Apollo, Minton's Playhouse, The Village Vanguard, The Blue Note, Sweet Basil's, The Five Spot, and Birdland.

Suggested Listening:

The Best of the Modern Jazz Quartet by the MJQ
A Night At Birdland (album) by Art Blakey
Duke at the Cotton Club (album) by Duke Ellington
Stompin' At the Savoy by Chick Webb

Theory Concept – *Jazz played in swing style in 3/4 time can have a variety of accents.*

196. RHYTHM WORKOUT

197. THEORY WORKOUT – Chord Vamp I and ii in Concert E♭

198. IMPROVISATION WORKOUT – Major Scale over I and ii Vamp

199. MELODY WORKOUT

SWING

ALTO SAX / BARITONE SAX

Doo Dot Bah Doo Doo Doo Doo Dot Doo Dot Bah Doo Doo Doo Doo

TENOR SAX

TRUMPET

TROMBONE

GUITAR

PIANO

BASS

BRUSHES

DRUMS

C TREBLE/ VIBES

A. SAX / B. SAX

Doo Dot Bah Doo Doo Doo Doo Dot Doo Dot Bah Doo Doo Doo Doo

T. SAX

TPT.

TBN.

GTR.

PNO.

BASS

DMS.

C/VIB.

A. SAX
B. SAX
T. SAX
TPT.
TBN.
GTR.
PNO.
BASS
DMS.
C/VIB.
Doo Dot
Doo Doo Doo
Doo Dot
Doo Doo Doo
Doo Dot
Doo Doo Doo
Doo Bah
Doo
A. SAX
B. SAX
T. SAX
TPT.
TBN.
GTR.
PNO.
BASS
DMS.
C/VIB.
Doo Dot Bah
Doo Doo Doo
Doo Dot
Doo Dot Bah
Doo Doo Doo
Doo

200. "SKATING IN THE PARK" – Full Band Arrangement

9
NO REPEAT ON D.S.
A. SAX
T. SAX
B. SAX
TPT.
TBN.
GTR.
PNO.
BASS
DMS.
C/VIB.
DIV.
mp
PLAY 2ND TIME AND ON D.S. ONLY
COMP
SIM.
EbMA9
FMI7/Eb
17

25
PLAY EACH TIME
A. SAX
T. SAX
B. SAX
TPT.
PLAY EACH TIME
TBN.
AbMA7
GM17
FM17
Bb7(b9)
GTR.
PNO.
BASS
DMS.
C/VIB.
33
TO CODA
PLAY 2ND TIME AND ON D.S. ONLY
PLAY 2ND TIME AND ON D.S. ONLY
DIV.
EbMA9
FM17/Eb

*CLEAR NOTEHEADS = CHORD TONES

201. DEMONSTRATION SOLO FOR "SKATING IN THE PARK"

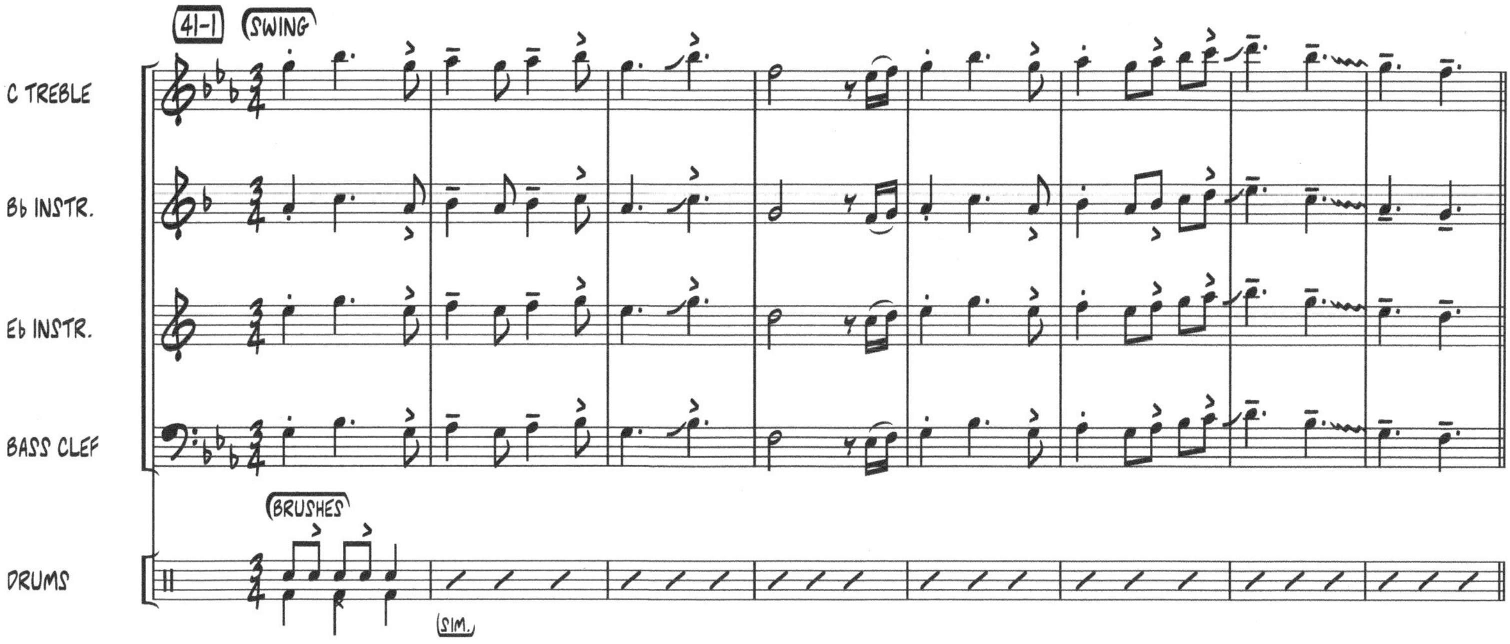
41-1
SWING
C TREBLE
Bb INSTR.
Eb INSTR.
BASS CLEF
BRUSHES
DRUMS
SIM.

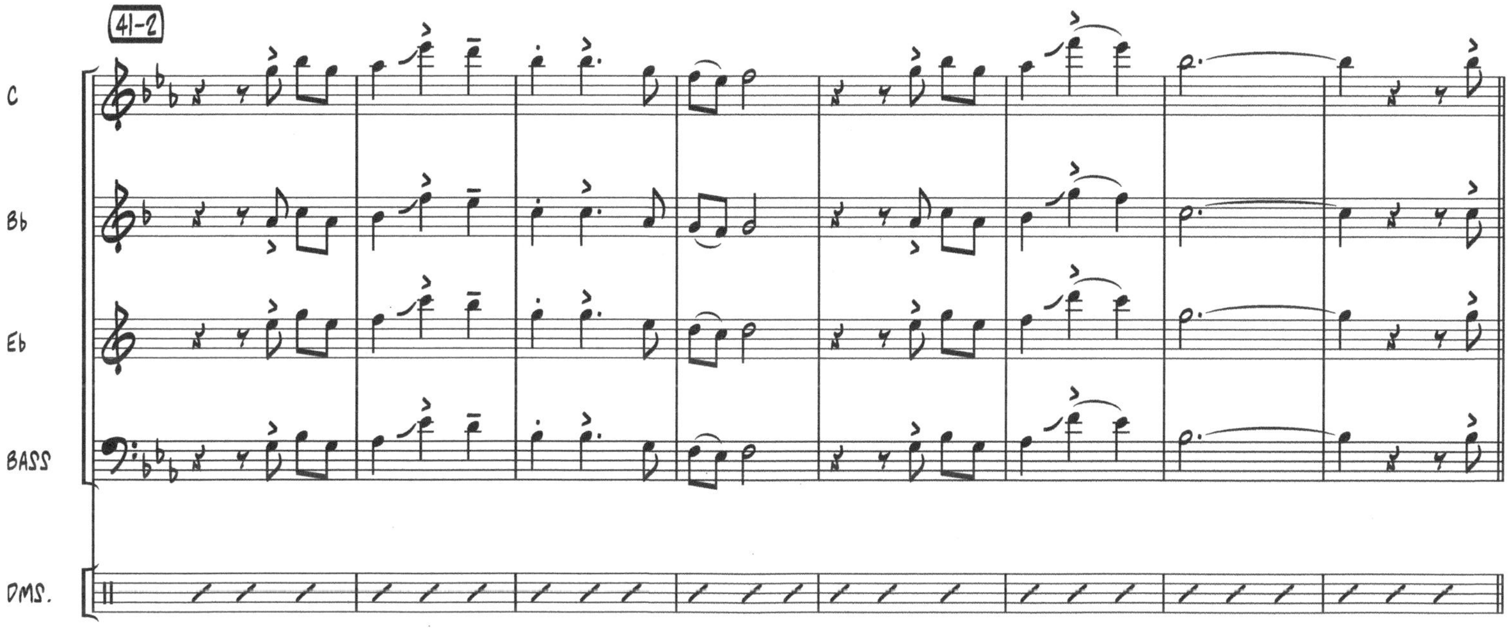
41-2
C
Bb
Eb
BASS
DMS.

41-3
C
Bb
Eb
BASS
DMS.

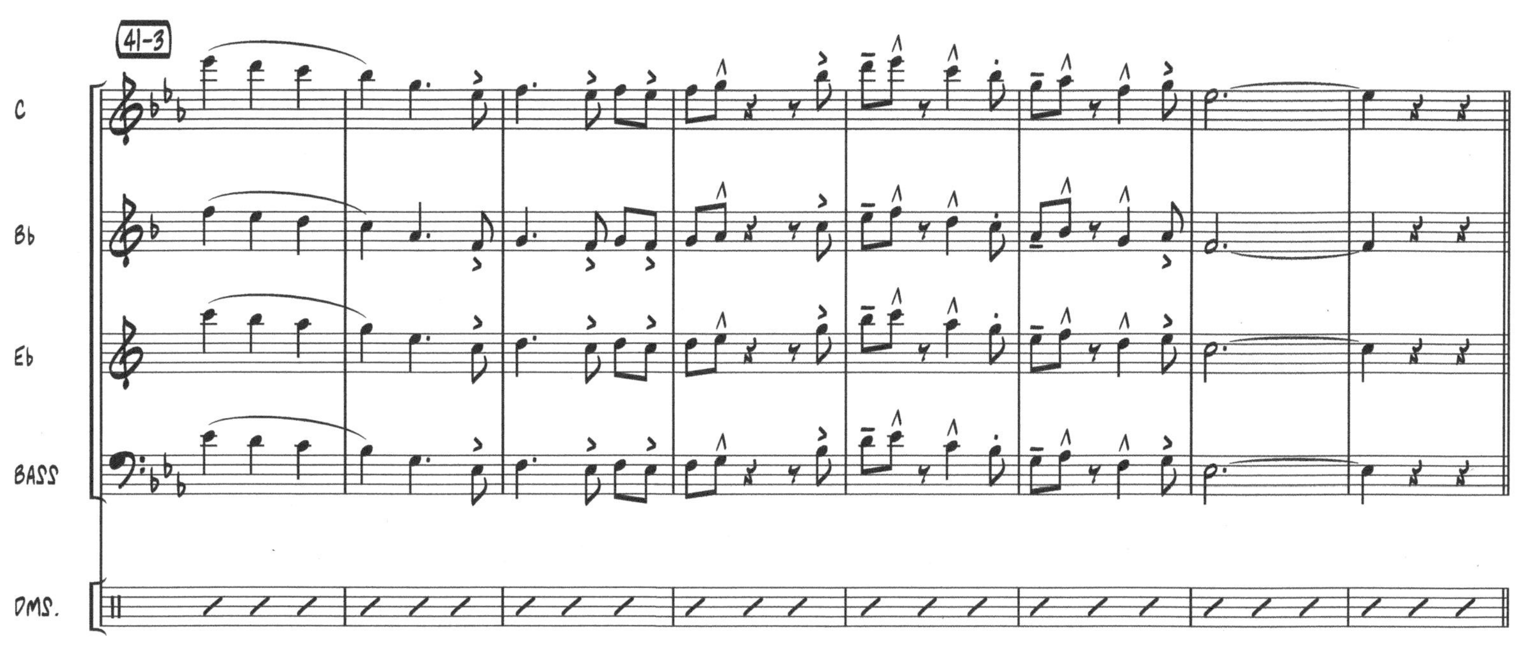

202. PRACTICE TRACK FOR "SKATING IN THE PARK" – mm. 41-48 (6 choruses)

Student Book Page 46

PERFORMANCE SPOTLIGHT *Five's A Crowd*

West Coast Jazz (often referred to as "Cool Jazz") is a style of jazz music that developed in the 1950s. West Coast Jazz was more sedate than bebop or hard bop. One of the most important recordings in this style is Dave Brubeck's *Time Out* which experimented with various time signatures. The most famous song from *Time Out* was "Take Five" by saxophonist Paul Desmond, which used the time signature of 5/4. Desmond was Brubeck's musical partner for many years. Important musicians associated with Cool Jazz or West Coast Jazz include:

Miles Davis	Gerry Mulligan	Dave Brubeck	Chet Baker	Lee Konitz
George Shearing	Shorty Rogers	Shelly Manne	Bud Shank	Art Farmer

Additional Teacher Information

Five's a Crowd – West Coast Jazz

West Coast Jazz (similar to "Cool Jazz") is a style that was developed in the 1950s in Los Angeles and San Francisco. It was more sedate than bebop or hard bop and became extremely popular. The Dave Brubeck Quartet typified the West Coast sound and Brubeck's album *Time Out* remains one of the best selling jazz albums of all time. Brubeck and his saxophonist Paul Desmond's experiments with jazz in time signatures other than the more common $\frac{4}{4}$ or $\frac{3}{4}$ were ground breaking at the time (1959). Today jazz musicians commonly use odd meters such as $\frac{7}{4}$, $\frac{7}{8}$, and $\frac{9}{4}$ in jazz songs.

Suggested Listening:

Time Out by The Dave Brubeck Quartet
Time Further Out by The Dave Brubeck Quartet
Chain Reaction by Don Ellis
Whiplash by Don Ellis
Hank's Opener by Stan Kenton
Time for a Change by Stan Kenton

203. RHYTHM WORKOUT

A. SAX
B. SAX

Doo Dot Bah Doo Dot | Doo Dot Doo Dot | Doo Bah Doo Dot Doo Dot | Doo Bah Doo Dot Bah Doo Dot

T. SAX

TPT.

TBN.

GTR.

PNO.

BASS

DMS.

C/VIB.

204. THEORY WORKOUT – Two Chord Vamp in Dorian

Listen, then play. Pick any note.

(SWING)

ALTO SAX
BARITONE SAX

AMI G AMI G AMI G AMI G

TENOR SAX

DMI C DMI C DMI C DMI C

TRUMPET

DMI C DMI C DMI C DMI C

TROMBONE

CMI Bb CMI Bb CMI Bb CMI Bb

GUITAR

CMI Bb CMI Bb CMI Bb CMI Bb

PIANO

CMI Bb CMI Bb CMI Bb CMI Bb

BASS

CMI Bb CMI Bb CMI Bb CMI Bb

DRUMS

C TREBLE/
VIBES

CMI Bb CMI Bb CMI Bb CMI Bb

205. IMPROVISATION WORKOUT #1 – Using the Dorian Mode Over the Two Chord Vamp

206. IMPROVISATION WORKOUT #2 – Chord Tones

Effective solos can be built using the chord tones.

207. MELODY WORKOUT

208. "FIVE'S A CROWD" – Full Band Arrangement

A. SAX
T. SAX
B. SAX
TPT.
TBN.
GTR.
PNO.
BASS
DMS.
C/VIB.
CMI7
SIM.
2
17
CMI7
F9
BbMA7
EbMA7
AbMA7
3

*CLEAR NOTEHEADS = CHORD TONES

A. SAX
T. SAX
B. SAX
TPT.
TBN.
GTR.
PNO.
BASS
DMS.
C/VIB.
AMI
G
DMI
C
CMI
Bb
CMI7
33
DIV.
f
CMI9
F9
BbMA7
EbMA7
AbMA7
FMI7
G13
D.C. AL CODA

CODA
1.
2.
A. SAX
T. SAX
B. SAX
TPT.
TBN.
GTR.
PNO.
BASS
DMS.
C/VIB.
DIV.
mp-f
GRAD. DIM.
CMI7
Bb

209. DEMONSTRATION SOLO FOR "FIVE'S A CROWD"

210. PRACTICE TRACK FOR "FIVE'S A CROWD" – mm. 25-32 (8 choruses)

Suggested Listening/Artist by Instrument

Voice
Louis Armstrong
Anita Baker
Chet Baker
Tony Bennett
George Benson
Nat King Cole
Harry Connick Jr.
Ruth Brown
Blossom Dearie
Kurt Elling
Ella Fitzgerald
Astrud Gilberto
Johnny Hartman
Billie Holiday
Peggy Lee
Kevin Mahogany
Bobby McFerrin
Anita O'Day
Lou Rawls
Jimmy Rushing
Frank Sinatra
Bessie Smith
Esperanza Spalding
Mel Tormé
Dinah Washington
Ethel Waters
Cassandra Wilson
Nancy Wilson

Soprano Saxophone
Sidney Bechet
Jane Ira Bloom
John Coltrane
Bill Evans
Steve Lacy
Dave Liebman
Joe Lovano
Branford Marsalis
Wayne Shorter

Alto Saxophone
Julian "Cannonball" Adderley
Benny Carter
Richie Cole
Ornette Coleman
Paul Desmond
Eric Dolphy
Paquito D'Rivera
Sonny Fortune
Gary Foster
Kenny Garrett
Antonio Hart
Johnny Hodges
Lee Kontiz
Jimmy Lunceford
Jackie McLean
James Moody
Oliver Nelson
Charlie Parker
David Sanborn
Bud Shank
Sonny Stitt
Bobby Watson
Phil Woods

Tenor Saxophone
Gene Ammons
Michael Brecker
John Coltrane
George Coleman
Bob Cooper
Eddie "Lockjaw" Davis
Hershel Evans
Joe Farrell
Bud Freeman
Stan Getz
Benny Golson
Dexter Gordon
Johnny Griffin
Coleman Hawkins
Jimmy Heath
Joe Henderson
Rahsaan Roland Kirk
Pat La Barbera
Yusef Lateef
Joe Lovano
Branford Marsalis
Hank Mobley
Bob Mintzer
Chris Potter
Sonny Rollins
Wayne Shorter
Zoot Sims
Sonny Stitt
Lew Tabackin
Lester Young
Ben Webster

Baritone Saxophone
Pepper Adams
Nick Brignola
Ronnie Cuber
Gerry Mulligan
Scott Robinson
Gary Smulyan

Trumpet
Nat Adderley
Ambrose Akinmusire
Red Allen
Louis Armstrong
Chet Baker
Bix Beiderbecke
Terence Blanchard
Buddy Bolden
Lester Bowie
Randy Brecker
Clifford Brown
Donald Byrd
Don Cherry
Buck Clayton
Miles Davis
Kenny Dorham
Roy Eldridge
Jon Faddis
Art Farmer
Dizzy Gillespie
Tim Hagans
Roy Hargrove
Tom Harrell
Freddie Hubbard
Harry James
Chuck Mangione
Wynton Marsalis
Lee Morgan
Fats Navarro
King Oliver
Hot Lips Page
Louis Prima
Red Rodney
Shorty Rogers
Arturo Sandoval
Doc Severinsen
Woody Shaw
Bobby Shew
Rex Stewart
Clark Terry
Kenny Wheeler

Trombone
Ray Anderson
Bob Brookmeyer
Jimmy Cleveland
Hal Crook
Michael Davis
Michael Dease
Vic Dickenson
Tommy Dorsey
Robin Eubanks
John Fedchock
Carl Fontana
Curtis Fuller
Wycliffe Gordon
Urbie Green
Al Grey
Wayne Henderson
Conrad Herwig
J. J. Johnson
Jimmy Knepper
Elliot Mason
Glenn Miller
Kid Ory
Jim Pugh
Julian Priester
Bill Reichenbach
Frank Rosolino
Jack Teagarden
Bill Watrous
Phil Wilson
Kai Winding

Guitar
John Abercrombie
Luiz Bonfà
Charlie Christian
Larry Coryell
George Benson
Kenny Burrell
Herb Ellis
Tal Farlow
Bill Frisell
Joao Gilberto
Freddie Green
Grant Green
Jerry Hahn
Jim Hall
Antonio Carlos Jobim
Stanley Jordan
Barney Kessel
Pat Martino
John McLaughlin
Pat Metheny
Wes Montgomery
Joe Pass
Les Paul
Django Reinhardt
Emily Remler
Kurt Rosenwinkel
John Scofield

Piano
Mose Allison
Kenny Barron
Count Basie
Joanne Brackeen
Dave Brubeck
George Cables
Chick Corea
Kenny Drew
Duke Ellington
Bill Evans
Red Garland
Vince Guaraldi
Herbie Hancock
Barry Harris
Ahmad Jamal
Dr. John
Keith Jarrett
Hank Jones
Wynton Kelly
John Lewis
Ramsey Lewis
Harold Mabern
Les McCann
Jay McShann
Brad Mehldau
Thelonious Monk
Jelly Roll Morton
Bennie Moten
Horace Parlan
Oscar Peterson
Bud Powell
Sun Ra
George Shearing
Horace Silver
Cecil Taylor
Art Tatum
Bobby Timmons
Lennie Tristano
McCoy Tyner
Mal Waldron
Fats Waller
Cedar Walton
Randy Weston
Mary Lou Williams
Teddy Wilson
Joe Zawinul

Suggested Listening/Artist by Instrument *(Cont.)*

Organ
Joey DeFrancesco
Jimmy McGriff
Shirley Scott
Jimmy Smith
Lonnie Smith

Bass
Steve Bailey
Keter Betts
Jimmy Blanton
Walter Booker
Ray Brown
Ron Carter
Paul Chambers
Stanley Clarke
John Clayton
Bob Cranshaw
Israel Crosby
Ray Drummond
George Duvivier
Pops Foster
Dave Friesen
Jimmy Garrison
Eddie Gomez
Charlie Haden
Percy Heath
Milt Hinton
Dave Holland
Robert Hurst
Chuck Israels
Marc Johnson
Scott LaFaro
Cecil McBee
Christian McBride
Marcus Miller
Charles Mingus
Buell Neidlinger
Walter Page
Jaco Pastorius
John Pattitucci
Gary Peacock
Oscar Pettiford
Lynn Seaton
Slam Stewart
Butch Warren
Victor Wooten
Reggie Workman
Eugene Wright

Drums
Carl Allen
Louie Bellson
Brian Blade
Art Blakey
Terri Lyne Carrington
Kenny Clarke
Jimmy Cobb
Billy Cobham
Jack DeJohnette
Peter Erskine
Al Foster
Steve Gadd
Jeff Hamilton
Billy Hart
Jake Hanna
Roy Haynes
J. C. Heard
Albert "Tootie" Heath
Billy Higgins
Elvin Jones
Jo Jones
Philly Joe Jones
Gene Krupa
Joe La Barbera
Mel Lewis
Shelly Manne
Harvey Mason
Airto Moriera
Paul Motian
Lewis Nash
Bernard Purdie
Buddy Rich
John Riley
Max Roach
Marvin "Smitty" Smith
Ed Soph
Grady Tate
Ed Thigpen
Jeff "Tain" Watts
Lenny White
Tony Williams

Percussion
Don Alias
Sammy Figueroa
Airto Moriera
Chano Pozo
Tito Puente
Poncho Sanchez
Mongo Santamaria

Vibes
Lionel Hampton
Stefon Harris
Bobby Hutchinson
Milt Jackson
Mike Marineri
Red Norvo
Dave Samuels (marimba)

Flute
Eric Dolphy
Joe Farrell
Paul Horn
Yusef Lateef
Hubert Laws
Charles Lloyd
Herbie Mann
James Newton
Bud Shank
Lew Tabackin
Dave Valentine
Jim Walker
Frank Wess

Clarinet
Don Byron
John Carter
Eddie Daniels
Buddy DeFranco
Paquito D'Rivera
Gary Foster
Benny Goodman
Ken Peplowski
Artie Shaw

Miscellaneous
David Amram (french horn)
Stephane Grappelli (violin)
Andy Kirk (tuba)
Paul McCandless (oboe)
Toots Thielemans (harmonica)
Julius Watkins (french horn)
Claude Williams (violin)

Credits

Author Mike Steinel

Managing Editor Michael Sweeney

Production Editor James Gagne

Music Engraving and Typesetting Thomas Schaller

Cover Photographs Brookfield Central H.S. Band, Brookfield, WI, Jason Gillette, Director

Recording Artists
Mike Steinel – Trumpet
Devin Eddleman – Alto Saxophone
John Murphy – Tenor Saxophone
Tony Baker – Trombone
Brian Piper – Piano
Paul Metzger – Guitar
Lynn Seaton – Bass
Steve Barnes – Drums

Recording and Mixing Engineer Reeltime Audio, Denton, TX Eric Delegard